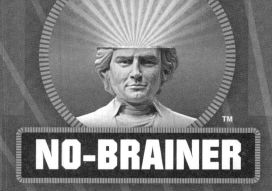

NO-BRAINER™

PLAY GUITAR

WE MAKE PLAYING GUITAR A NO-BRAINER!

Alfred

SINCE 1922

Alfred Music Publishing Co., Inc. • P.O. Box 10003 • Van Nuys, CA 91410-0003

alfred.com

ISBN-10: 0-7390-6251-4 (Book & DVD)
ISBN-13: 978-0-7390-6251-7 (Book & DVD)

Guitar photos (left to right) courtesy of Gibson Musical Instruments and Taylor Guitars • Beethoven bust photo courtesy of www.Statues.com

 Printed on 100% recycled paper.

2

CONTENTS

About the Authors 5

Part 1: The Basics 6

The Parts of the Guitar. 6

Choosing a Guitar 6
   Steel Strings and Nylon Strings

How to Hold Your Guitar 7

The Right Hand 8
   Strumming with a Pick
   Strumming with Your Fingers

The Left Hand 9
   Proper Left-Hand Position
   Placing a Finger on a String

Tuning Your Guitar 10
   Using the DVD
   Tuning the Guitar to Itself
   Pitch Pipes and Electronic Tuners

The Basics of Reading Music 11
   The Staff
   The Treble Clef
   Measures (Bars)
   Reading TAB
   Chord Diagrams

Notes on the First String E 14
   Playing E, F and G on My Extra Fine Guitar
   Extra Credit

Counting Time 16
   Four Kinds of Notes
   Time Signatures

Repeat Signs 17
   Blues in C

Notes on the Second String B. 18
   Jammin' on Two Strings
   Beautiful Brown Eyes
   Blues in G
   Rockin' Guitar

Jingle Bells. 22

Two-String Blues 23

Notes on the Third String G 24
   Jammin' on Three Strings
   Largo from the New World Symphony
   Aura Lee

Three-String Boogie 27

Chords 28
   Two-Note Exercise
   Three-Note Chord Exercise

Three-String C Chord 29

Ode to Joy 30

Three-String G7 Chord 31
   Love Somebody
   Jammin' with Two Chords

Three-String G Chord. 34
   She'll Be Comin' 'Round the Mountain

Notes on the Fourth String D 36
   Old MacDonald Had a Farm
   Reuben Reuben
   C Blues

Daisy Bell 38

Four-String Dance 40

Four-String G & G7 Chords. 41
   Rock Me Mozart!

Notes on the Fifth String A 43
   Volga Boatmen
   A Minor Boogie

Five-String Blues. 45

High A. 46
   Back in Russia

Incomplete Measures 47
   A-Tisket, A-Tasket
   The Yellow Rose of Texas

Notes on the Sixth String E 49
   All the Notes You've Learned So Far

Tempo Signs. 50
   Three-Tempo Rock
   Theme from Carmen

Metallic Rock 51

Bass-Chord Accompaniment. 52

Can-Can (duet). 53

Dynamics 54
   Theme from Beethoven's Fifth Symphony

Half Rests & Whole Rests 56
   Give It a Rest

Four-String C Chord 57
   When the Saints Go Marching In

Ties 58
   Shenandoah

More Bass-Chord Accompaniments . . 60
   Cielito Lindo

Eighth Notes. 62
   Jammin' with Eighth Notes
   Walkin' with Eighths

Crescendo & Diminuendo 64
   Pachelbel's Canon

Sharps ♯, Flats ♭, and Naturals ♮ 66

3

The Chromatic Scale 67
Chromatic Rock

Four-String D7 Chord 69
Blues in G

Amazing Grace 70

Rockin' the Bach 71

Rockin' Up 'n' Down 72

The Major Scale 73
C Major Scale

Key Signatures 74
The Key of C Major
The Key of G Major
The Key of F Major

Eighth Rests 75

La Bamba 76

$\frac{2}{4}$ Time Signature 78
Bill Bailey

Dotted Quarter Notes 80
Auld Lang Syne

Hava Nagila 82

Key of C Major 84
C Major Scale
Three Chords in C Major
Accompaniment in C Major

Two-Octave C Major Scale 86
Joy to the World

Three-String F Minor Chord 88
Home on the Range

Variation on Little Brown Jug 90

Cut Time 92
Variation on Jim Crack Corn

Key of G Major 94
G Major Scale
The Three Principal Chords in G Major
Tiritomba

Shortnin' Bread 96

Key of A Minor 97
Two-Octave A Harmonic Minor Scale
The Three Principal Chords in A Minor
Accompaniments in A Minor

Four-String F Chord 99
Bass-Chord Accompaniment in the
   Key of C Major

The Entertainer 100

Part 2: Rock Guitar 102

Rockin' With Chords 102
The Six-String E Chord
The Four-String D Chord
Rhythmic Notation
Dig In the Chords

The Five-String A Chord 103
Talking 'Bout My Baby #1
Two-String Talking 'Bout My Baby

Power Chords 104
The Five-String C Chord
Four-Chord Rock

More Power Chords 106
6th-String-Root Power Chords
5th-String-Root Power Chords

D. C. al fine and Form 108
Shakin' the Rafters

Eighth Notes in Rhythmic Notation . . 109
Lead and Alchemy

Movable Chords 110
E-Major-Shape Barre Chords
A-Major-Shape Barre Chords

You Got Me Rockin' 112

Comin' Around 113

Reading Fingerboard Scale Diagrams . . 114

Basic Concepts Review 115
The Major Scale
Triads and Diatonic Harmony

The Minor Pentatonic Scale 116
E Minor Pentatonic Scale Fingerings
A Minor Pentatonic Scale Fingerings
Hammer-Ons and Pull-Offs

The Blues Scale 118
G Blues Scale Fingerings
Eighth-Note Triplets
G Blues/Rock Solo

12-Bar Blues Forms 120
12-Bar Blues in C
12-Bar Blues in C Variation

You Ain't Got a Soul to Sell 121

Choosing Which Scale to Use 122
Solo in D

The Major Pentatonic Scale 123
C Major Pentatonic Scale Fingerings

4

Slides 124
   Sliding, Slithery Snake
   When it Rains, It's Red
   Sixteenth Notes
   Malodorous Mama

Phrasing Tips 127
   Rhythmic Imitation
   Wheelin' and Stealin'
   Using Rests Effectively
   Varying Dynamics and Tone
   Exploring Full Range of Pitch
   Up and Down Your Spine

Rock Technique 131
   Bending
   Grace Notes
   Vibrato
   Prepare to Launch
   Quarter-Step bends

**Rock Licks in the
   Styles of the Masters** 135
   In the Style of Eric Clapton
   In the Style of Jimi Hendrix
   In the Style of Jimmy Page
   In the Style of Carlos Santana
   In the Style of Kirk Hammett

Jam Tracks 140
   Slash Notation

J. B. Goode's Blues 141

K. C.'s Blues 142

Eddie's Rock 143

Dorian Rock 144

Phrygian Rock 145

Jeff's Jam 146

**Part 3: Being a Professional
   Guitarist** 147

**Finding, Rehearsing and
   Promoting a Band** 147
   How to Tell if You're Ready to
     Play in a Band
   How to Start a Band
   How to Find and Get Into
     an Existing Band
   How to Be the One Everyone
     Wants in Their Band

   Your Personal Promotional Pack
   How to Prepare for an Audition
   Rehearsing and Improving the Band
   How to Get Gigs for Your Band
   The Gig

Get Better, Sooner 155
   Getting Warmed Up
   Practicing
   Getting Out of a Rut

**A Few Things You Need to Know
   About the Music Biz** 160
   Getting What's Coming to You
   Career Tips
   Getting a Record Contract
   Performance Contract
   True Stories

Part 4: Reference 164

Changing Strings 164
   Removing Strings
   Attaching New Strings
   Classical Guitar Tie-On Bridge
   Classical Guitar—Tie-On Tuning Pegs

Chord Theory 168
   Intervals
   Table of Intervals

Basic Triads 170

Building Chords 171

The Circle of Fifths 173

Chord Symbol Variations 174

Reading Chords 175

Chord Dictionary 176

Guitar Fingerboard Chart 224

About the DVD

The DVD contains valuable demonstrations of all the instructional material in Part 1. You will get the best results by following along with your book as you watch these video segments. Musical examples that are not performed with video are included as audio tracks on the DVD for listening and playing along. The audio tracks are all accesible through the chapter selection on your DVD player and also as downloadable mp3 files on your computer.

ABOUT THE AUTHORS

The Meeting of Great Minds

In order to enlighten you, we have gathered a standout roster of authors who specialize in different facets of teaching guitar. Every one of them contributes to making guitar playing a no-brainer. Here is a little information on each of them.

Joe Bouchard

Joe is one of the founding members, and bassist, of the legendary rock band Blue Öyster Cult. Currently, Joe performs and teaches guitar, bass, and piano. He is the author of many instructional books and videos published by the National Guitar Workshop and Alfred Music Publishing.

L. C. Harnsberger

L. C. Harnsberger studied music composition at the University of Southern California. Since finishing school, he has been composing and performing as well as writing best-selling instructional books. His *Kid's Guitar Course* (co-written with Ron Manus) has received numerous awards and continues to grow in popularity. Other publications include guitar methods, reference books and, performance music for band and orchestra. He is currently the editor-in-chief of the Musical Instruments division at Alfred Music Publishing.

Jason Kokoszka

Jason is a guitarist/bassist/composer who studied at Massachusetts College of Liberal Arts. In addition to a career performing music, Jason has contributed to the educational field. He wrote an instructional method on rock guitar soloing and teaches for the music-education website WorkshopLive.com.

Paul Lidel

By the time Paul signed his first major-label recording contract at age 23, he had already been playing professionally since age 14. Paul has over 2,000 shows under his belt, having toured abroad and performing in 45 states in the U.S. Paul's latest project had him recording and performing with the band Dangerous Toys. In addition to performing, Paul also enjoys teaching guitar at the University of Texas and has been on the faculty of the National Guitar Workshop.

Ron Manus

Ron is co-owner of Alfred Music Publishing and its sister company, Daisy Rock Guitars. He is one of Alfred Music's most prolific and top-selling authors, with over 100 published titles to his credit. Ron has written instructional books for guitar, bass, banjo, harmonica, and ukulele. In addition to holding prominent positions with Alfred and Daisy Rock, Ron also plays guitar and sings in the rock-solid, no-nonsense, punk-rock band sASSafrASS.

Other Important Contributors

The play-along tracks and licks in the style of famous artists were contributed by Chris Amelar, Tomas Cataldo, and Robert Brown. All three are all top-level performers, educators, and composers and have served as faculty members at the prestigious National Guitar Workshop.

PART 1: THE BASICS

VIDEO EXAMPLE

THE PARTS OF THE GUITAR

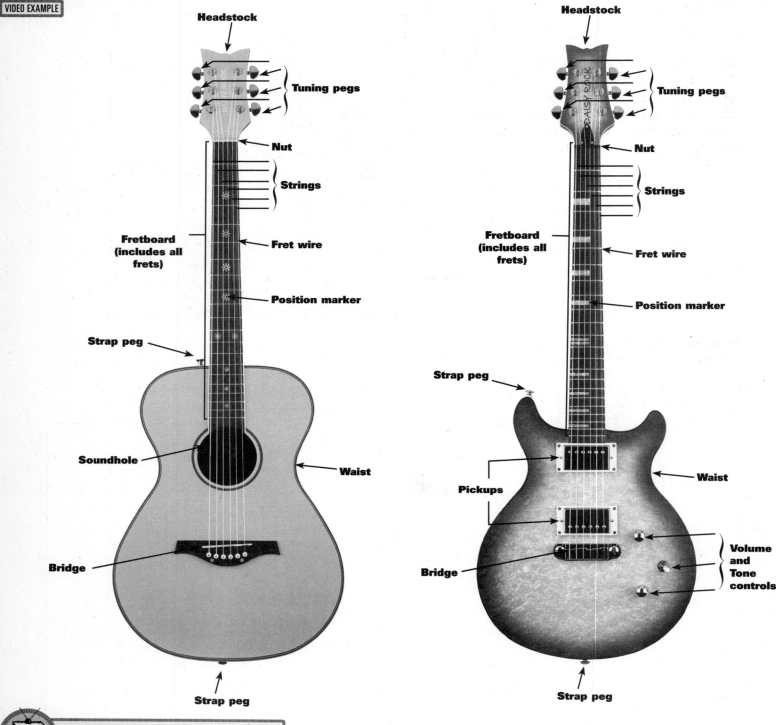

VIDEO EXAMPLE

CHOOSING A GUITAR

Steel Strings and Nylon Strings

Steel strings are found on both acoustic and electric guitars.
They have a bright and brassy sound.

Nylon strings are usually found on classical and flamenco guitars.
They have a mellow, delicate sound. Nylon strings are often easier for
beginners to play because they are easier on the fingers than steel strings.

HOW TO HOLD YOUR GUITAR

Below are three ways to hold your guitar.
Pick the one that is most comfortable for you.

When playing, keep your left wrist away
from the fingerboard. This will allow
your fingers to be in a better position
to finger the chords. Press your fingers
firmly, but make certain they do not
touch the neighboring strings.

Sitting.

Sitting with legs crossed.

Standing with strap.

THE RIGHT HAND

To *strum* means to play the strings with your right hand by brushing quickly across them. There are two common ways of strumming the strings. One is with a pick, and the other is with your fingers.

Strumming with a Pick

Hold the pick between your thumb and index finger. Hold it firmly, but don't squeeze it too hard.

Strum from the sixth string (the thickest, lowest-sounding string) to the first string (the thinnest, highest-sounding string).

Start near the top string.

Move mostly your wrist, not just your arm. Finish near the bottom string.

TIPS

Important: Strum by mostly moving your wrist, not just your arm. Use as little motion as possible. Start as close to the top string as you can, and never let your hand move past the edge of the guitar.

Strumming with Your Fingers

First, decide if you feel more comfortable strumming with the side of your thumb or the nail of your index finger. The strumming motion is the same with the thumb or finger as it is when using the pick. Strum from the sixth string (the thickest, lowest-sounding string) to the first string (the thinnest, highest-sounding string).

Strumming with the thumb.

Strumming with the index finger.

Let's Strum

Strum all six strings slowly and evenly. Count your strums out loud as you play. Repeat this exercise until you feel comfortable strumming the strings.

strum	strum	strum	strum	strum	strum	strum	strum
/	/	/	/	/	/	/	/

Count: 1   2   3   4   5   6   7   8

VIDEO EXAMPLE

THE LEFT HAND

Proper Left-Hand Position

Learning to use your left-hand fingers starts with a good hand position. Place your hand so your thumb rests comfortably in the middle of the back of the neck. Position your fingers on the front of the neck as if you are gently squeezing a ball between them and your thumb. Keep your elbow in and your fingers curved.

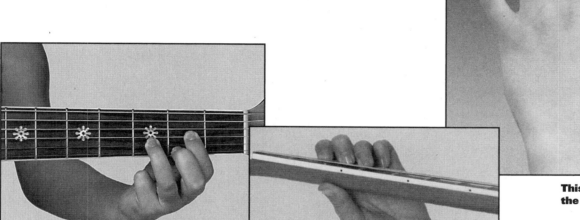

This is how the fingers of the left hand are numbered.

Keep elbow in and fingers curved.

Like gently squeezing a ball between your fingertips and thumb.

Placing a Finger on a String

When you press a string with a left-hand finger, make sure you press firmly with the tip of your finger and as close to the fret wire as you can without actually being right on it. Short fingernails are important! This will create a clean, bright tone.

RIGHT
Finger presses the string down near the fret without actually being on it.

WRONG
Finger is too far from fret wire; tone is "buzzy" and indefinite.

WRONG
Finger is on top of fret wire; tone is muffled and unclear.

TUNING YOUR GUITAR

First, make sure your strings are wound properly around the tuning pegs. They should go from the inside to the outside as illustrated to the right. Some guitars have all six tuning pegs on the same side of the headstock. If this is the case, make sure all six strings are wound the same way, from the inside out.

Turning a tuning peg clockwise makes the pitch lower. Turning a tuning peg counter-clockwise makes the pitch higher. Be sure not to tune the strings too high because they could break.

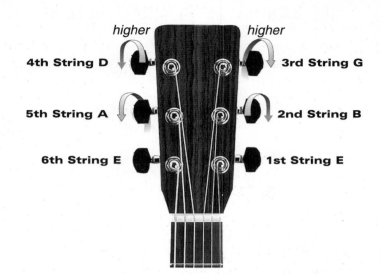

Important:

Always remember that the thinnest, highest-sounding string, the one closest to the floor, is the first string. The thickest, lowest-sounding string, the one closest to the ceiling, is the sixth string. When guitarists say "the highest string," they are referring to the highest-sounding string.

The six strings of your guitar are the same pitch as the six notes shown on the piano in the following illustration:

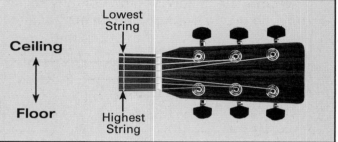

Using the DVD

When tuning while watching the DVD, listen to the directions and match each of your guitar's strings to the corresponding pitches.

Tuning the Guitar to Itself

When your sixth string is in tune, you can tune the rest of the strings using the guitar alone. First, tune the sixth string to E on the piano:

Then, follow the instructions below to get the guitar in tune.

Press 5th fret of 6th string to get pitch of 5th string (A).

Press 5th fret of 5th string to get pitch of 4th string (D).

Press 5th fret of 4th string to get pitch of 3rd string (G).

Press 4th fret of 3rd string to get pitch of 2nd string (B).

Press 5th fret of 2nd string to get pitch of 1st string (E).

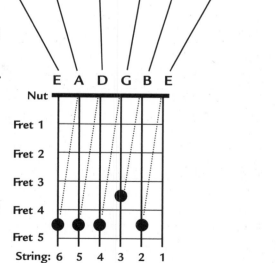

DID YOU KNOW?

Pitch Pipes and Electronic Tuners

If you don't have a piano available, consider buying an electronic tuner or pitch pipe. There are many types available, and a salesperson at your local music store can help you decide which is best for you.

THE BASICS OF READING MUSIC

Musical sounds are indicated by symbols called *notes.*
Their time value is determined by their color (white or black)
and by stems or flags attached to the note.

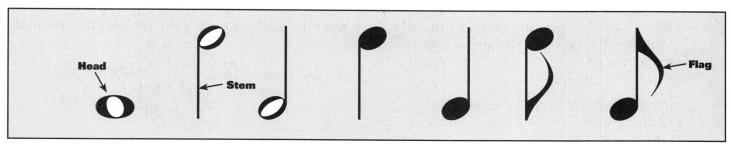

The Staff

The notes are named after the first seven letters of the alphabet (A–G), which are repeated
to embrace the entire range of musical sound. The name and pitch of a note are determined
by the note's position on five horizontal lines and four spaces between called the *staff.*

5th LINE
4th LINE — 4th SPACE
3rd LINE — 3rd SPACE
2nd LINE — 2nd SPACE
1st LINE — 1st SPACE

The Treble Clef

During the evolution of musical notation, the staff had from 2 to
20 lines, and symbols were invented to locate certain lines and the
pitch of the note on that line. These symbols were called *clefs.*

Music for the guitar is written in the *G clef* or *treble clef.* Originally the Gothic letter G
was used on a four-line staff to establish the pitch of G.

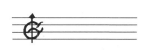

This grew into the modern
symbol we use today:

Treble Clef

G

Notes on the lines — Notes in the spaces

E G B D F   F A C E

Measures (Bars)

Music is also divided into equal parts
called *measures* or *bars.* One measure
is divided from another by a *bar line*:

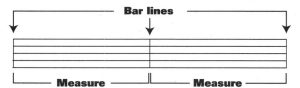

Bar lines

Measure   Measure

The Quarter Note

A quarter note equals one count.

Reading TAB

All the music in this book is written two ways: in standard music notation and in *TAB*.

Below each standard music staff you'll find a six-line TAB staff. Each line represents a string of the guitar, with the highest, thinnest string at the top and the lowest, thickest string at the bottom.

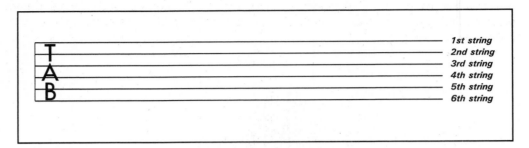

Numbers placed on the TAB lines tell you which fret to play.
A zero means to play the string open (not fingered).

1st string	2nd string	3rd string	4th string
3rd fret	1st fret	open	2nd fret

Numbers placed one on top of the other are played at the same time.

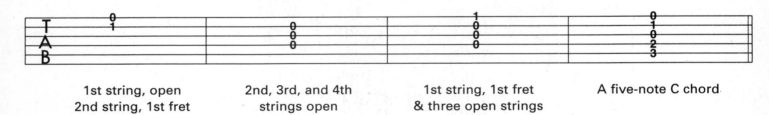

1st string, open	2nd, 3rd, and 4th	1st string, 1st fret	A five-note C chord
2nd string, 1st fret	strings open	& three open strings	

By glancing at the TAB, you can immediately tell where to play a note. Although you can't tell exactly what the rhythm is from the TAB, the horizontal spacing of the numbers gives you a strong hint about how long or short the notes are to be played.

Chord Diagrams

Chord diagrams are used to indicate fingering for chords. The example to the right means to place your first finger on the 1st fret, 2nd string, and second finger on the 2nd fret, 4th string. Then strum the first four strings only. The x's on the 5th and 6th strings indicate not to play these.

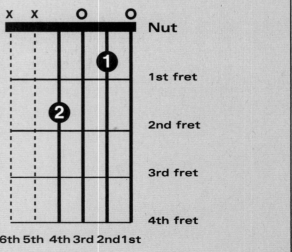

With a penchant for outrageous stage antics like lighting his guitar on fire, Jimi Hendrix was one of the most influential guitarists of his generation. Though he lived only a short life, his place in history as one of rock's greatest legends is solidified by his amazing technique and brilliant songwriting.

Photo: Courtesy of Reprise Records.

NOTES ON THE FIRST STRING E

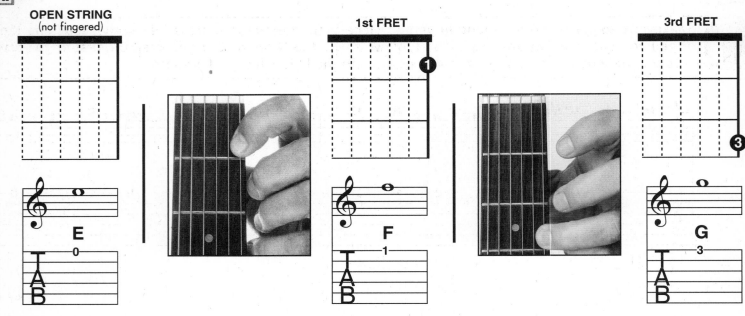

Play this example slowly and evenly. Use downstrokes for all this music.

Go to the next line without stopping.

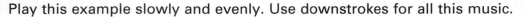

A *double bar line* indicates the end of a piece.

Playing E, F and G on My Extra Fine Guitar

Extra Credit

Make sure to place your left-hand fingers as close to the fret wires as possible without touching them. When you play the F on the 1st fret and follow it with the G on the 3rd fret, keep the first finger down. You will only hear the G, but when you go back to the F, it will sound smooth.

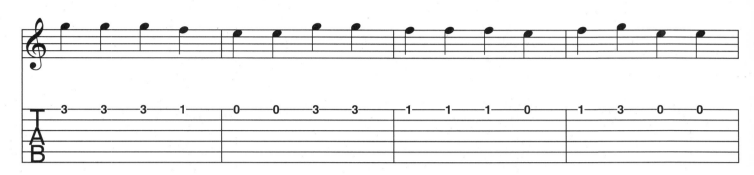

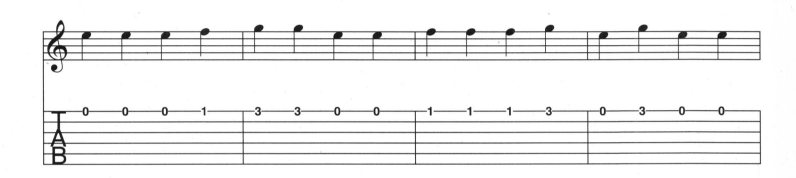

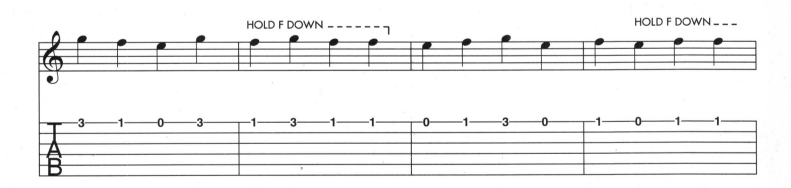

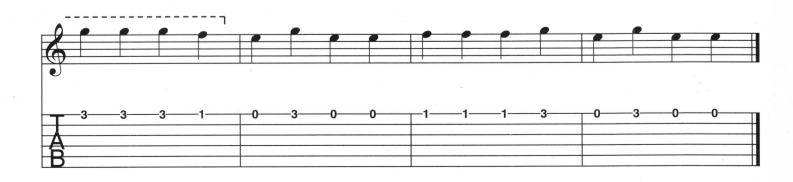

COUNTING TIME

Four Kinds of Notes

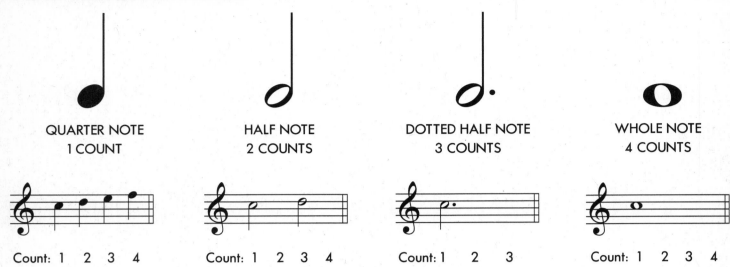

| QUARTER NOTE 1 COUNT | HALF NOTE 2 COUNTS | DOTTED HALF NOTE 3 COUNTS | WHOLE NOTE 4 COUNTS |

Count: 1 2 3 4   Count: 1 2 3 4   Count: 1 2 3   Count: 1 2 3 4

Time Signatures

Each piece of music has numbers at the beginning called a *time signature*.
These numbers tell us how to count time.

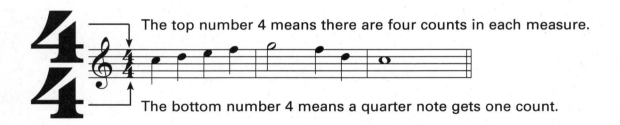

The top number 4 means there are four counts in each measure.

The bottom number 4 means a quarter note gets one count.

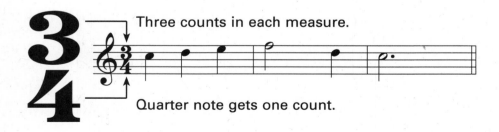

Three counts in each measure.

Quarter note gets one count.

IMPORTANT: Fill in the missing time signatures of the songs you already learned.

REPEAT SIGNS

This music uses *repeat signs.* The double dots inside the double bars tell you that everything between those double bars is to be repeated.

The best way to learn all the songs and exercises is to listen to the recording first so that you can hear exactly what is going to happen. Follow along in the music as you listen. Then, enjoy playing along.

Blues in C

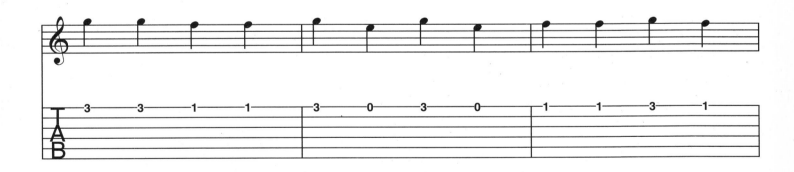

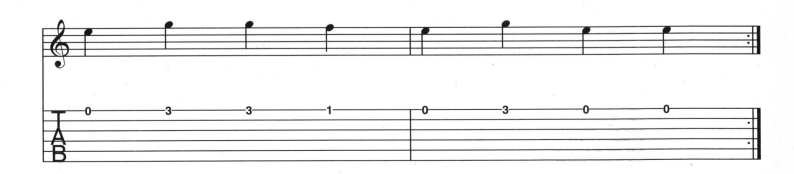

NOTES ON THE SECOND STRING B

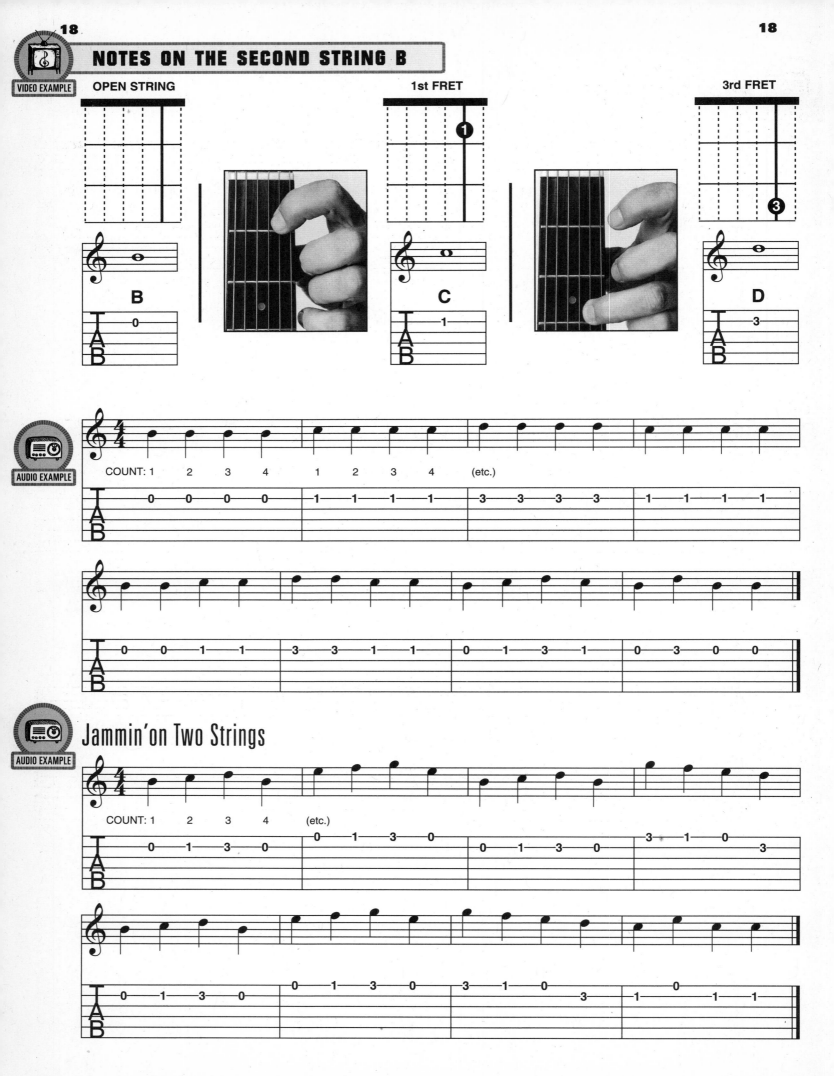

AUDIO EXAMPLE

Beautiful Brown Eyes

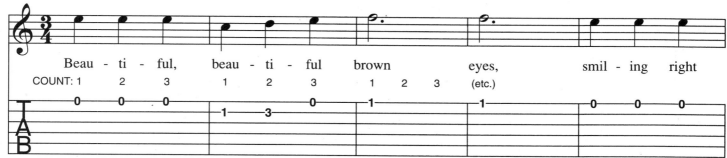

Beau - ti - ful, beau - ti - ful brown eyes, smil - ing right

COUNT: 1 2 3 1 2 3 1 2 3 (etc.)

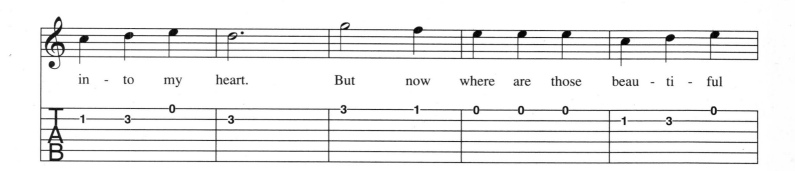

in - to my heart. But now where are those beau - ti - ful

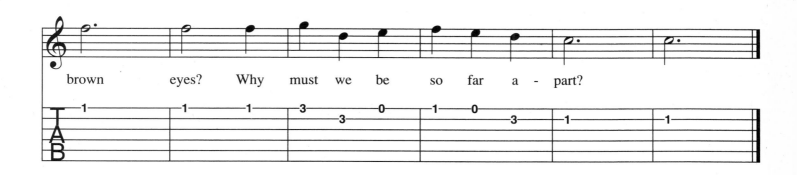

brown eyes? Why must we be so far a - part?

Blues in G

Chords for your teacher to play, or being played on the DVD:

Photo: Courtesy of the Institute of Jazz Studies

DID YOU KNOW?

Buddy Guy (born George "Buddy" Guy) is a Grammy Award-winning American blues and rock guitarist and singer. An inspiration to such great guitarists as Jimi Hendrix, Eric Clapton, and Stevie Ray Vaughan, he is considered an important exponent of Chicago blues. His career declined during the 1960s, but it finally took off again during the blues revival period of the late 1980s and early 1990s, sparked by Clapton's request that Guy be part of the "24 Nights" all-star blues guitar lineup at London's Royal Albert Hall and his subsequent signing with Silvertone Records.

Letters called *chord symbols* that are placed above each staff may be used for a duet. Either have a friend or teacher play the chords while you play the notes, or play along with the audio tracks on the DVD. Many of the tunes in the rest of this book include chords for duets.

Rockin' Guitar

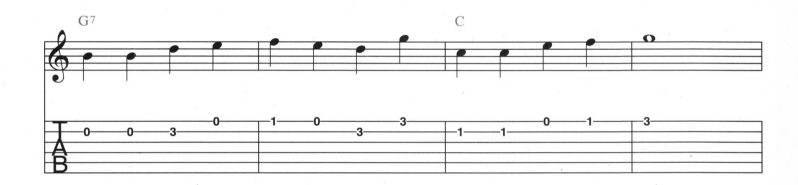

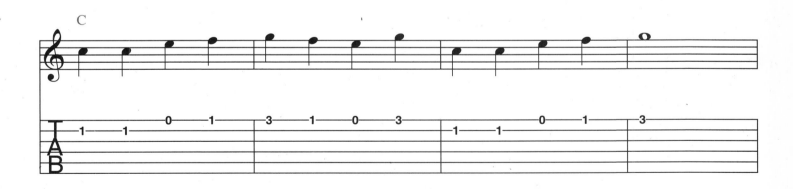

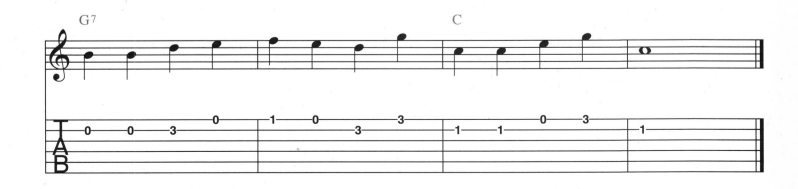

Jingle Bells

DUET: C

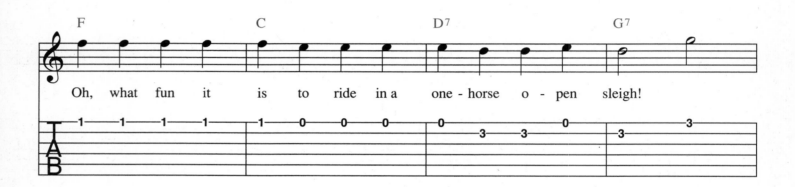

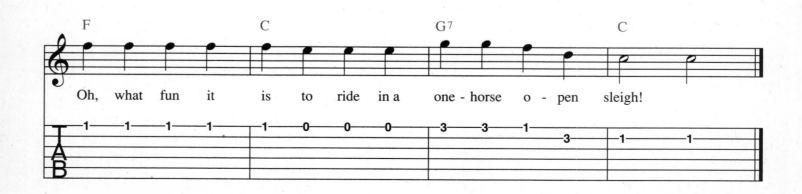

"Two-String Blues" uses all the notes we have learned so far: the notes on the 2nd string—B, C and D; and the notes on the 1st string—E, F and G.

Two-String Blues

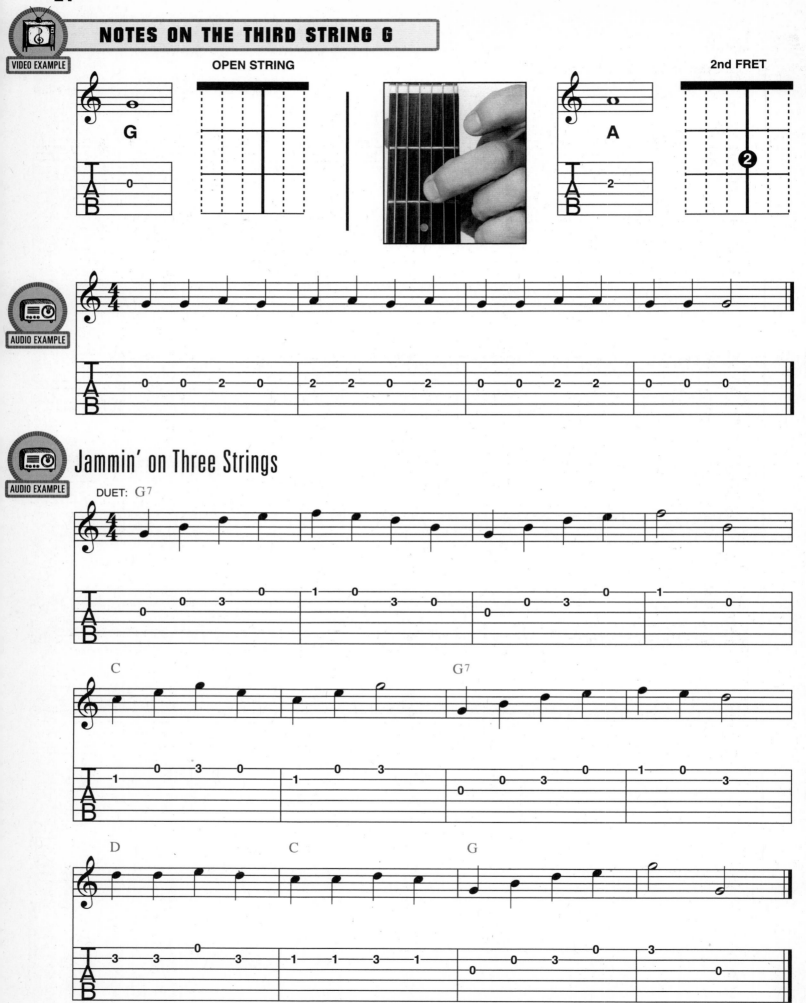

NOTES ON THE THIRD STRING G

VIDEO EXAMPLE

AUDIO EXAMPLE

Jammin' on Three Strings

AUDIO EXAMPLE

DUET: G7

Largo
from the New World Symphony

Dvořák

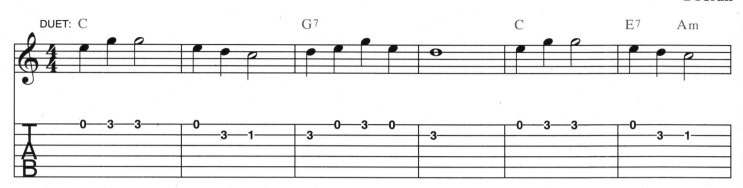

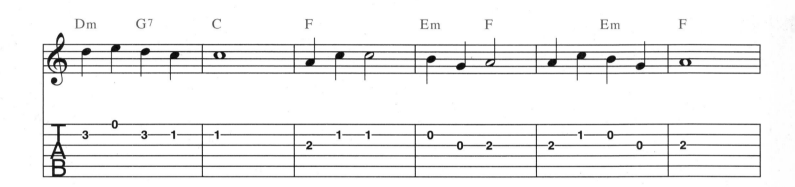

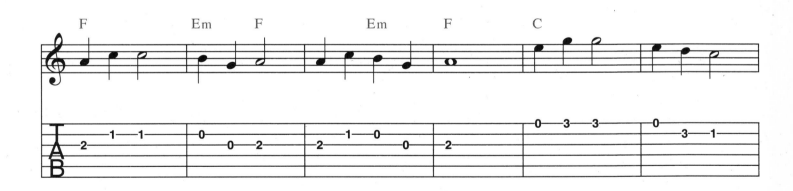

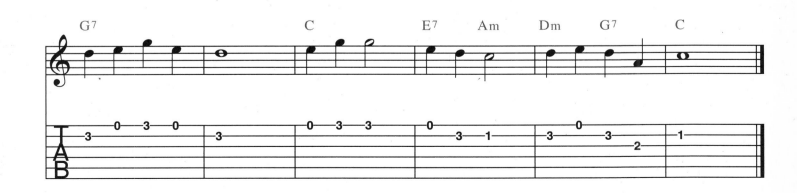

"Aura Lee" is an old American folk song that was later recorded by Elvis Presley and called "Love Me Tender."

AUDIO EXAMPLE

Aura Lee

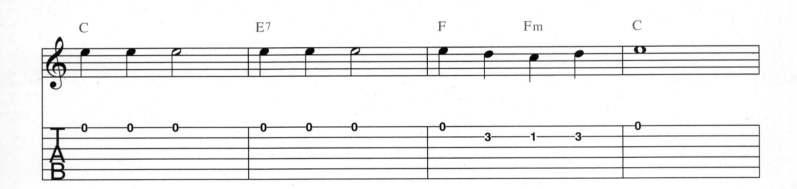

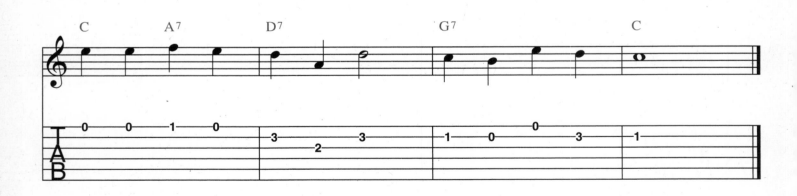

"Three-String Boogie" uses all the notes on all three strings that we have learned.
Don't forget to listen to the DVD audio first!

AUDIO EXAMPLE

Three-String Boogie

CHORDS

A *chord* is a combination of three or more notes played at the same time. All the notes are connected by a stem unless they are whole notes, which have no stem. The stems can go either up or down.

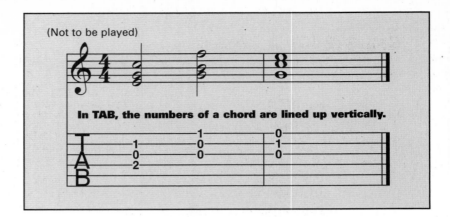

(Not to be played)

In TAB, the numbers of a chord are lined up vertically.

Two-Note Exercise

This exercise will get you used to playing two notes at a time—open B and open E.
Play both strings together with one down-stroke.

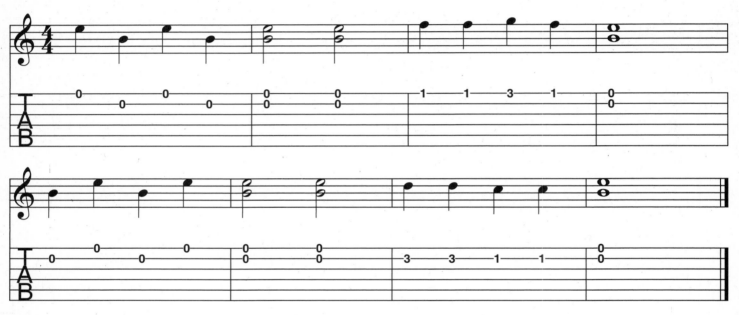

Three-Note Chord Exercise

This is the first time you are playing three-note chords.
All the chords in this exercise are made up of the open G, B and E strings.
Play it with your wrist free and relaxed. Remember to keep your eyes on the notes and not your hands.

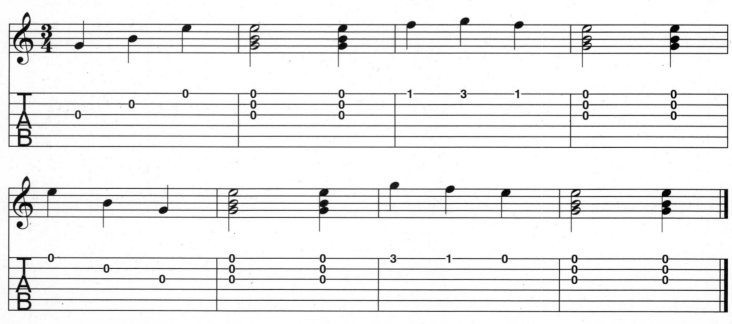

THREE-STRING C CHORD

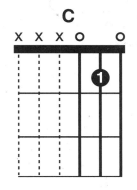
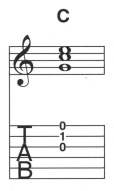

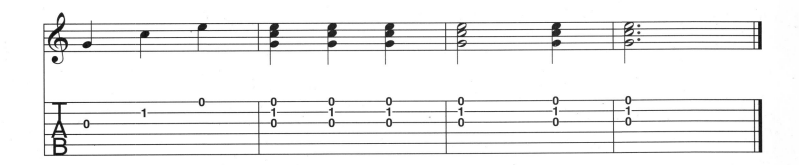

Eric Johnson is widely accepted as one of the most influential and gifted guitarists of the twentieth century. Born in Austin, Texas, he was only 16 when his immense talent was recognized, and by 21 he'd begun playing in legendary bands that came to include the Electromagnets, the Eric Johnson Group, and Avenue. After naming him Best Overall Guitarist for four consecutive years, *Guitar Player* magazine inducted him into their Gallery of Greats in 1995.

Photo: Ken Settle

VIDEO EXAMPLE

The Quarter Rest

It tells you to be silent for one count.

To make the rest very clear, stop the sound of the strings by touching the strings lightly with the heel of your right hand.

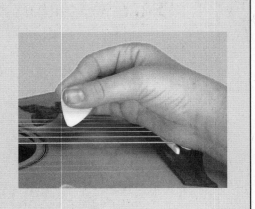

AUDIO EXAMPLE

Ode to Joy

Theme from Beethoven's Ninth Symphony

Beethoven

THREE-STRING G⁷ CHORD

Love Somebody

PLAY: C   G⁷   C   G⁷

SING: Love some-bod-y, 'deed I do. Love some-bod-y, now guess who?

C   G⁷   C G⁷ C

Love some-bod-y, have you guessed? You're the one that I love best.

Jammin' with Two Chords

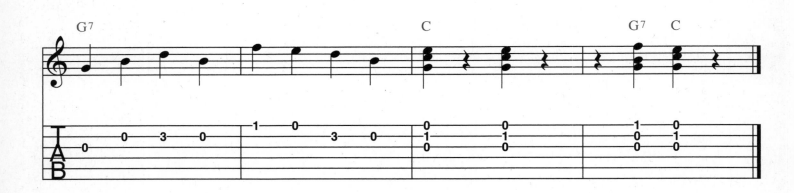

Dubbed the "King of Rock and Roll," Elvis Presley influenced several generations of young people to play guitar and may have had more impact on contemporary culture than any other figure in music.

Photo: Used by permission, Elvis Presley Enterprises, Inc.

THREE-STRING G CHORD

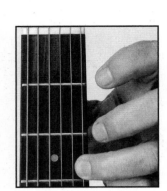

G

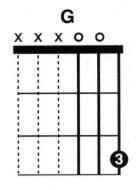

G

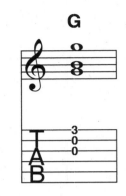

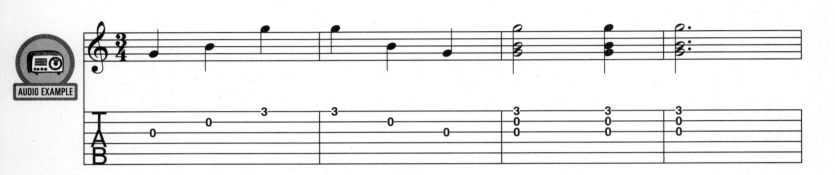

DID YOU KNOW?

One of the giants of rock 'n' roll, from his first records with The Beatles through his successful solo career, John Lennon played a major role in shaping pop music into what it is today. His combination of graceful melodies, unusual chord progressions and literate, sometimes biting, lyrics set a new standard for songwriting that continues to inspire fans around the world.

AUDIO EXAMPLE

She'll Be Comin' 'Round the Mountain

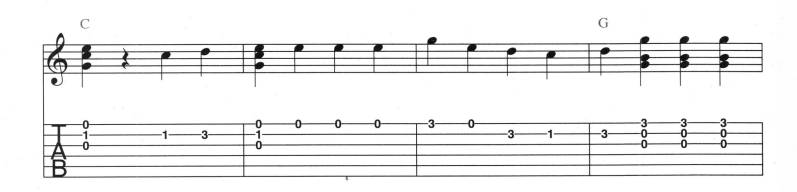

NOTES ON THE FOURTH STRING D

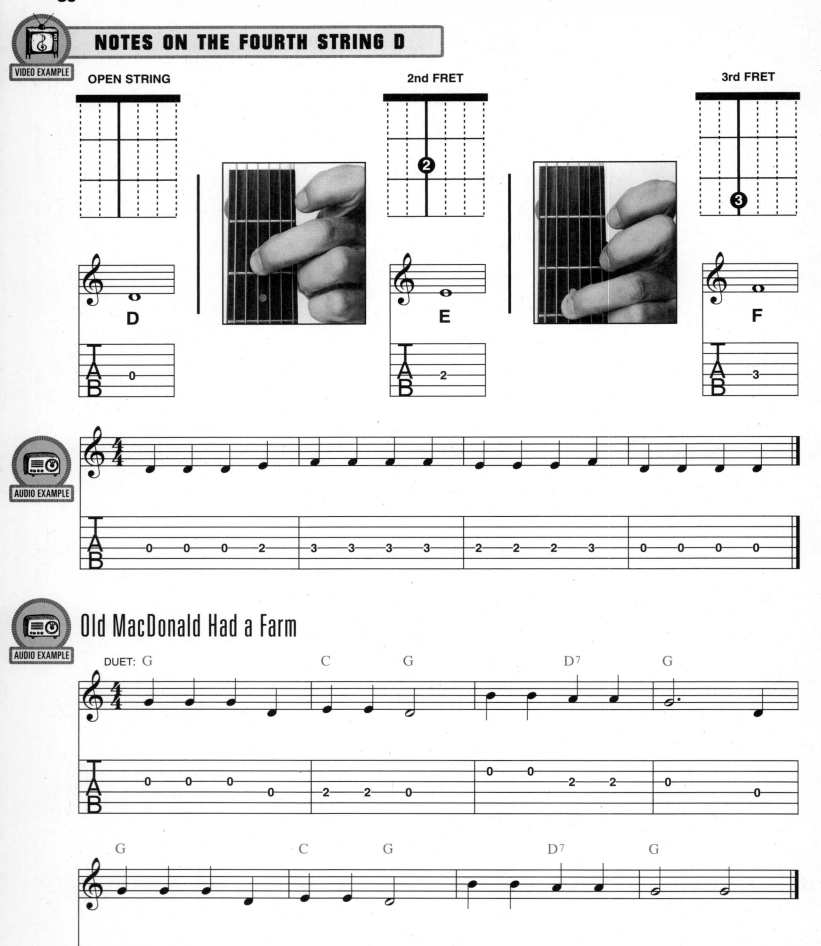

Old MacDonald Had a Farm

Reuben Reuben

"Reuben Reuben" uses a fermata (𝄐), which is also called a hold sign or pause sign. This sign tells you to lengthen the value of the note (usually twice its normal value).

C Blues

𝄴 stands for common time, which is the same as 4/4 time.

Now that you are getting better at playing chords, here is a song that will be lots of fun to play. In "Daisy Bell," you will be going from one note, to two notes, to three notes.

Daisy Bell

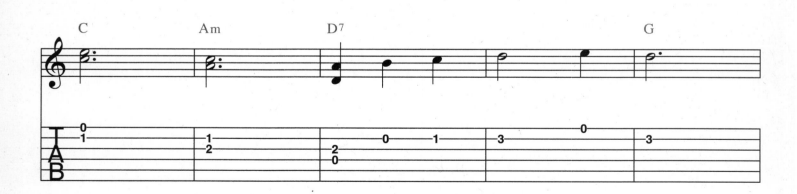

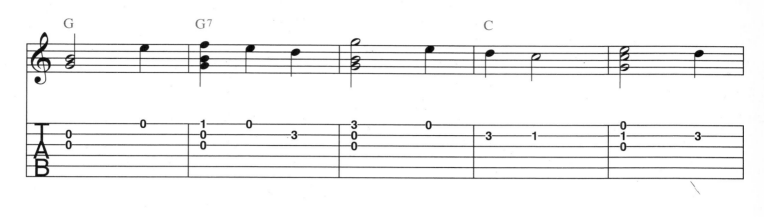

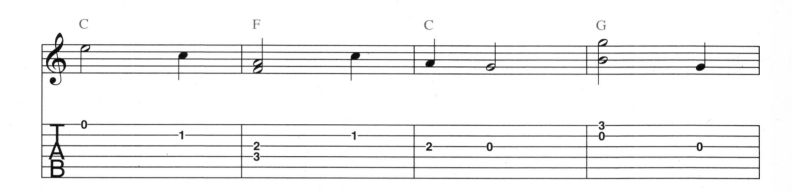

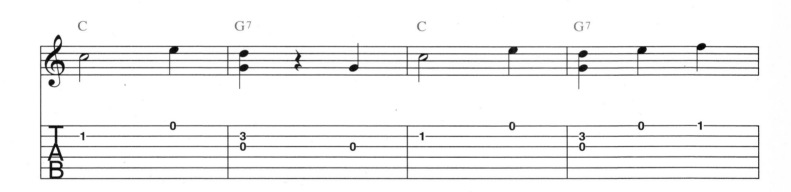

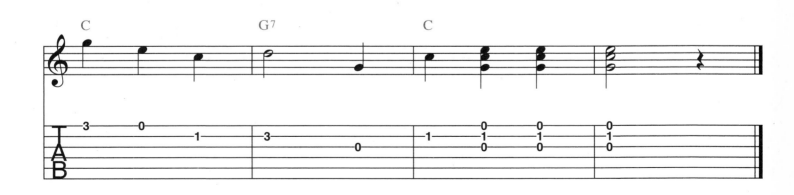

"Four-String Dance" has a jazzy feel. You will hear the melody played for you the first time through, then you are on your own with the band backing you up!

Four-String Dance

FOUR-STRING G & G⁷ CHORDS

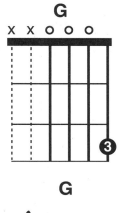

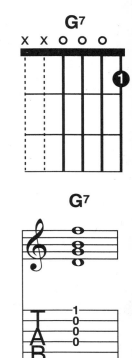

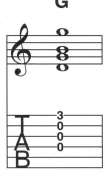

Although these new chords have the same names as chords you have already learned, they use four notes and sound more full.

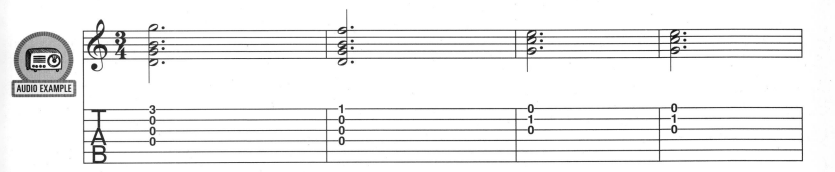

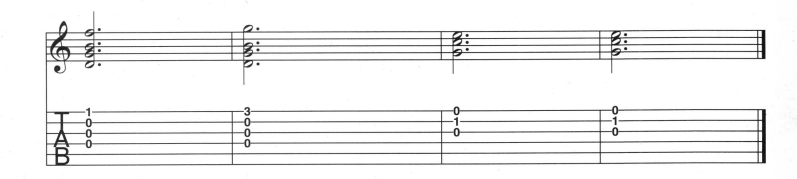

Rock Me Mozart!

Mozart

DUET: C

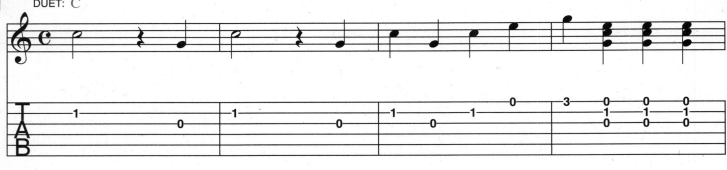

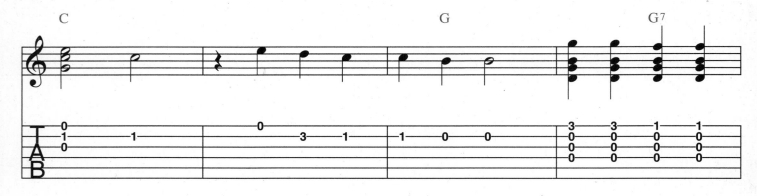

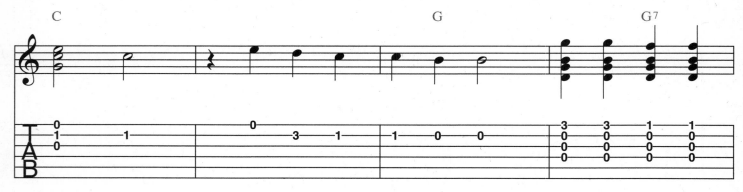

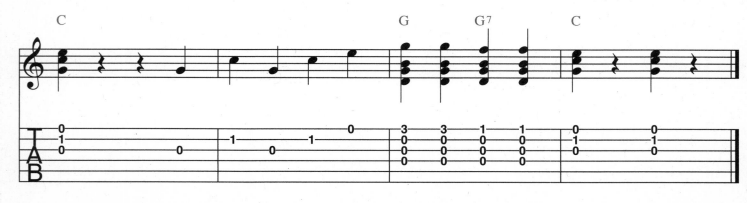

NOTES ON THE FIFTH STRING A

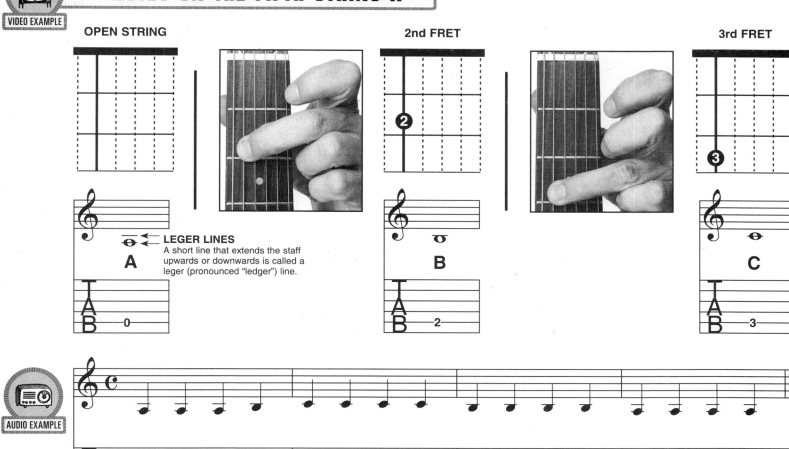

OPEN STRING

LEGER LINES
A short line that extends the staff upwards or downwards is called a leger (pronounced "ledger") line.

A

2nd FRET

B

3rd FRET

C

Volga Boatmen

DUET: Am   Dm   Am   Dm   Am

F   C   G   Am   Dm   Am

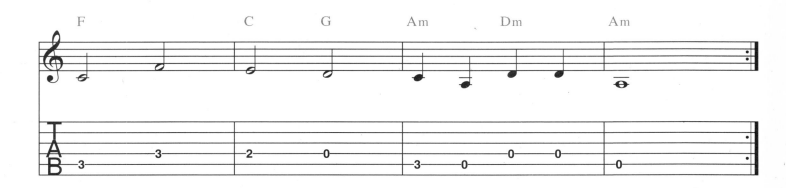

A Minor Boogie

Listen to the melody being played the first time through the tune. Then the tune will repeat three more times, with you as the lead guitarist.

Five-String Blues

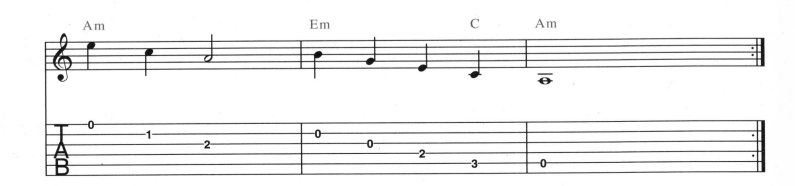

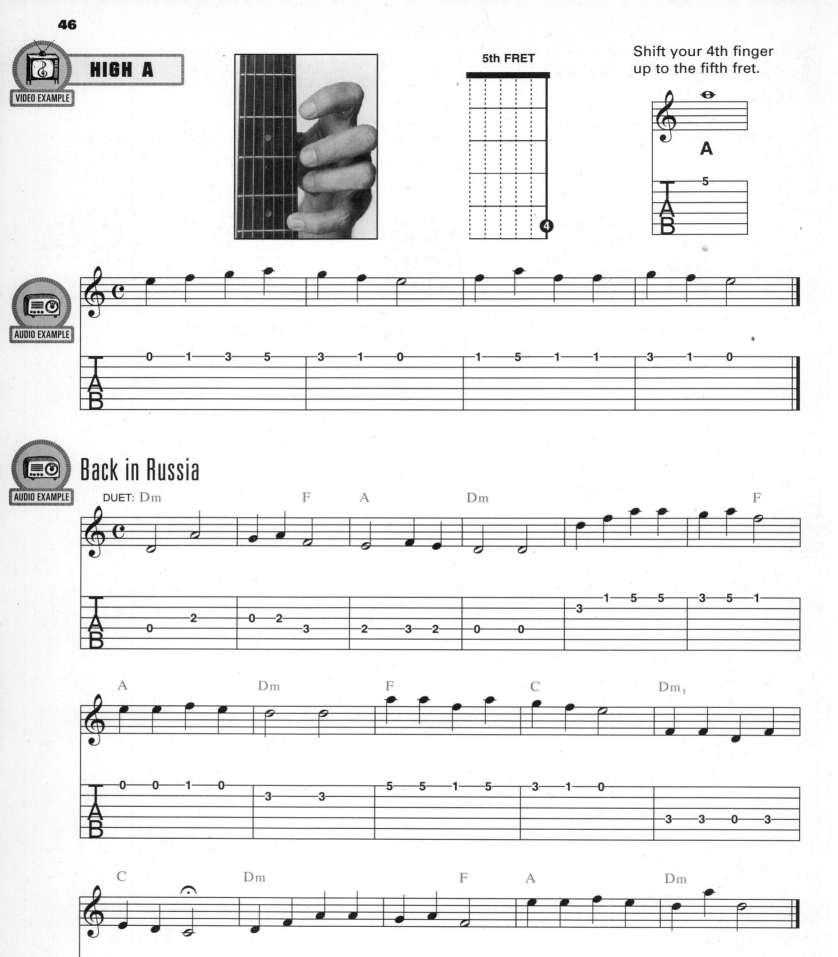

HIGH A

VIDEO EXAMPLE

5th FRET

Shift your 4th finger up to the fifth fret.

AUDIO EXAMPLE

Back in Russia

AUDIO EXAMPLE

DUET: Dm

INCOMPLETE MEASURES

Not all pieces of music begin on the first beat.
Sometimes, music begins with an incomplete measure called a pickup.
If the pickup is one beat, often the last measure will only have three beats in $\frac{4}{4}$, or two beats in $\frac{3}{4}$.

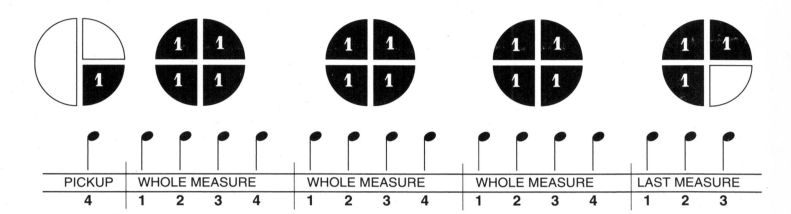

PICKUP	WHOLE MEASURE				WHOLE MEASURE				WHOLE MEASURE				LAST MEASURE		
4	1	2	3	4	1	2	3	4	1	2	3	4	1	2	3

A-Tisket, A-Tasket

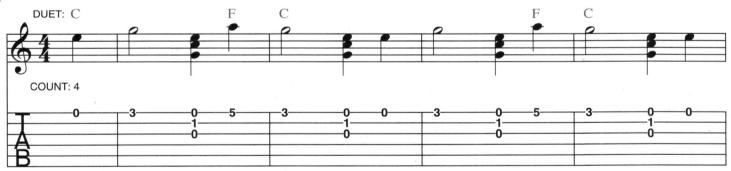

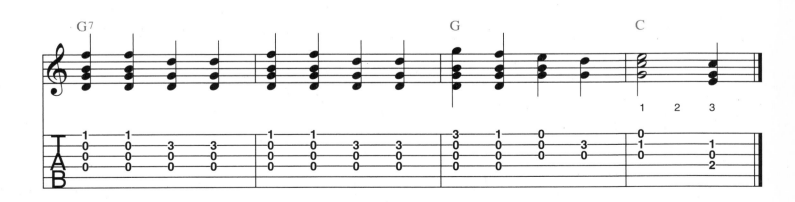

The Yellow Rose of Texas

DID YOU KNOW?

Texas guitarist Stevie Ray Vaughan brought the blues to an entire generation of music lovers and was admired by the likes of Eric Clapton, David Bowie and Buddy Guy for his extraordinary skill. Tragically, a plane crash claimed the life of this celebrated guitar legend in 1990.

Photo: Robert Knight

VIDEO EXAMPLE

NOTES ON THE SIXTH STRING E

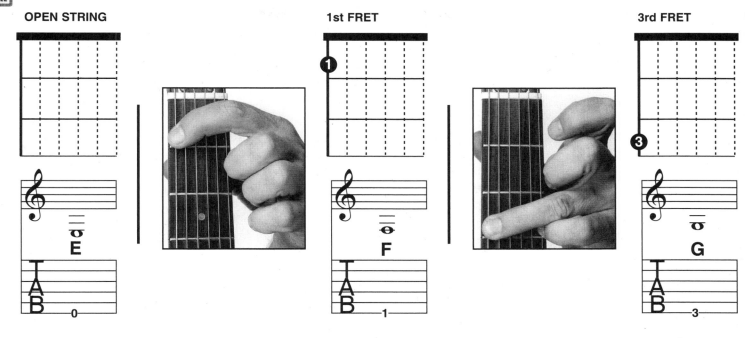

OPEN STRING   1st FRET   3rd FRET

E   F   G

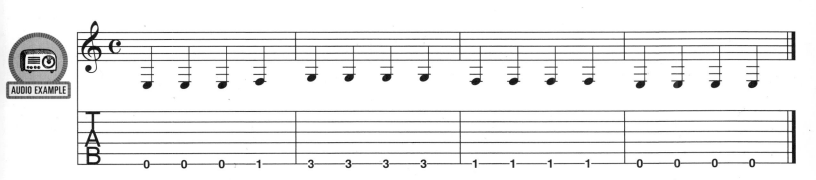

AUDIO EXAMPLE

VIDEO EXAMPLE

All the Notes You've Learned So Far

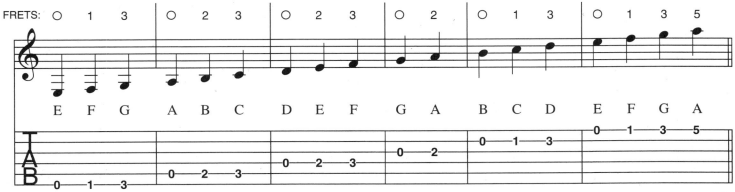

FRETS: 0   1   3 | 0   2   3 | 0   2   3 | 0   2 | 0   1   3 | 0   1   3   5

E   F   G   A   B   C   D   E   F   G   A   B   C   D   E   F   G   A

TEMPO SIGNS

VIDEO EXAMPLE

A *tempo* sign tells you how fast to play music.

The three most common tempo signs:

Andante (SLOW)

Moderato (MODERATELY)

Allegro (FAST)

AUDIO EXAMPLE

Three-Tempo Rock   Play three times: 1st time **Andante**, 2nd time **Moderato**, 3rd time **Allegro**.

Theme from Carmen

AUDIO EXAMPLE

You play the melody with the DVD audio track in this hard driving rock tune. This one uses almost every note you know on all six strings. Listen to the DVD audio first, and play the second and thrid times through!

Metallic Rock

BASS-CHORD ACCOMPANIMENT

A popular style of playing chord accompaniments in $\frac{4}{4}$ time breaks the chord into two parts: a single bass note followed by a chord made up of the remaining notes. On the 1st beat, play only the lowest note (called the *bass note*). Then play the rest of the chord (usually the three highest strings) on the 2nd, 3rd and 4th beats. The complete pattern is called **bass-chord-chord-chord**.

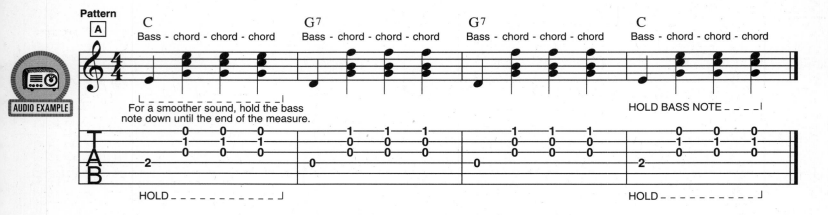

Another style of playing chord accompaniments in $\frac{4}{4}$ time uses a bass note on the 1st and 3rd beats and three-string chords on the 2nd and 4th beats. This is called **bass-chord-bass-chord**.

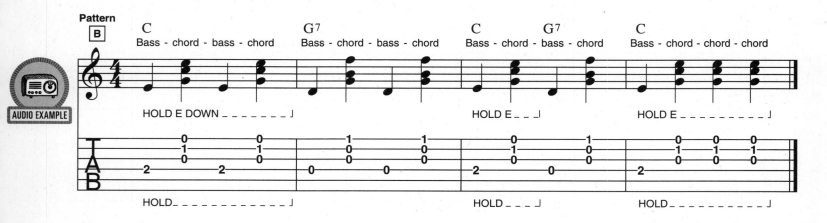

This style of playing chord accompaniments can be adapted to $\frac{3}{4}$ time by playing a bass note on the 1st beat and three-string chords on the 2nd and 3rd beats. This is called **bass-chord-chord**.

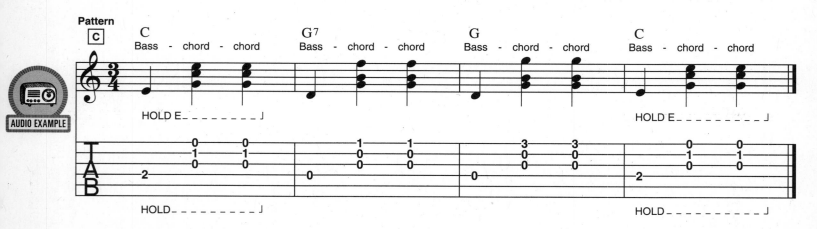

Can-Can (duet)

This famous melody is from the opera "Orpheus in the Underworld" by Jacques Offenbach.

You should learn this two different ways: First, play the solo part as written. Second, have a friend or teacher play the solo part, or listen to it on the DVD while you play a chord accompaniment using either pattern A or B from page 52.

Offenbach

DYNAMICS

Symbols that show how soft or loud to play are called *dynamics*. These symbols come from Italian words. The four most common dynamics are shown here:

𝆏 piano (SOFT)   **𝆐𝆑** mezzo-forte (MODERATELY LOUD)   **𝆑** forte (LOUD)   **𝆑𝆑** fortissimo (VERY LOUD)

Theme from Beethoven's Fifth Symphony

Beethoven

HALF RESTS & WHOLE RESTS

An easy way to remember the difference between the half and whole rest is to think of the whole rest as being longer (or heavier) and so hangs below the line. The half rest is shorter (or lighter) and so sits on top of the line.

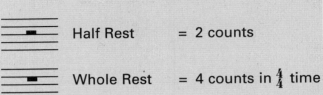

Half Rest = 2 counts

Whole Rest = 4 counts in 4/4 time

= 3 counts in 3/4 time } for a whole measure

Give It a Rest

Allegro moderato (Moderate Rock & Roll)

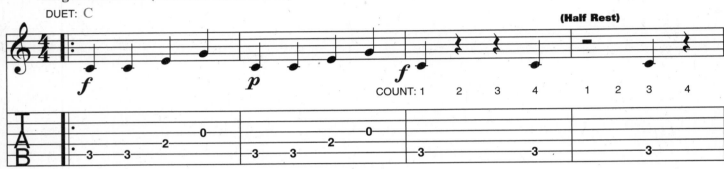

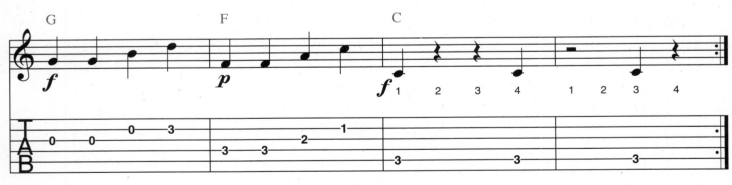

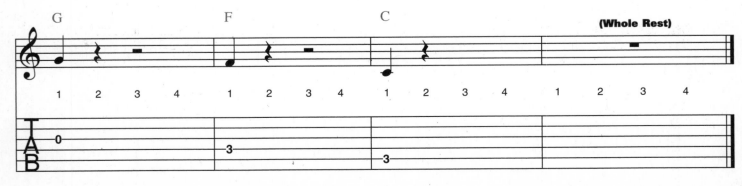

FOUR-STRING C CHORD

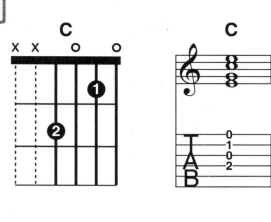

When the Saints Go Marching In

Allegro

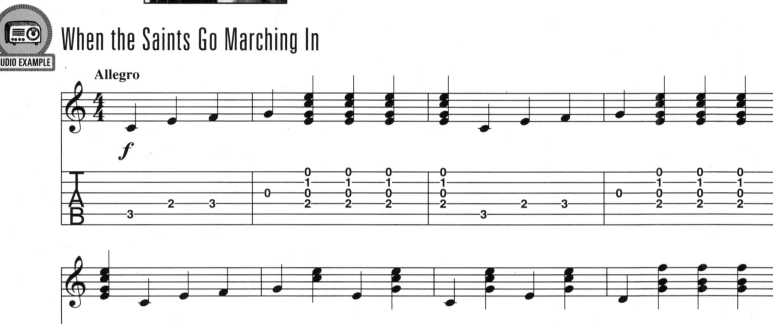

HOLD F DOWN _ _ _ _ _ |

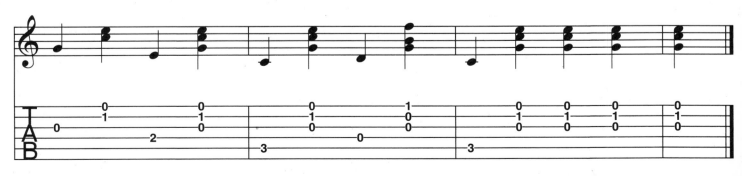

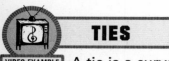

TIES

A tie is a curved line that joins two or more notes of the same pitch. When two notes are tied, the second is not played separately, but its value is instead added to the first note.

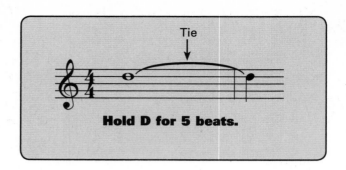

Two Quarter Notes, Tied   **Two Half Notes, Tied**

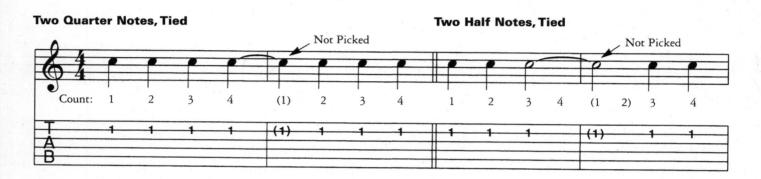

In TAB notation, the tie is often indicated by parentheses around the fret number. Do not pick that note again.

Whole Note Tied to a Quarter Note   **Tied Notes in $\frac{3}{4}$ Time**

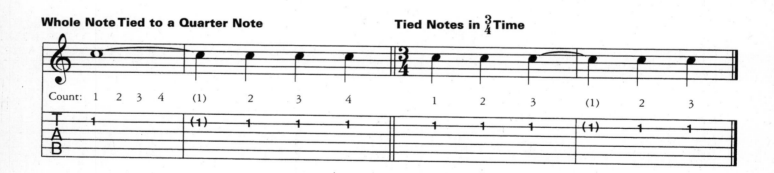

Shenandoah

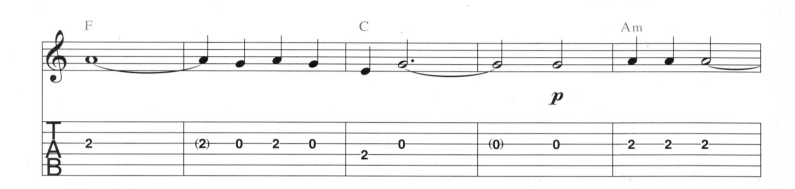

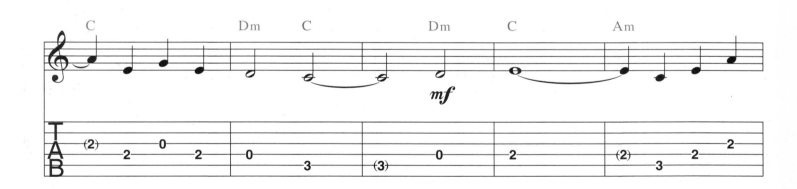

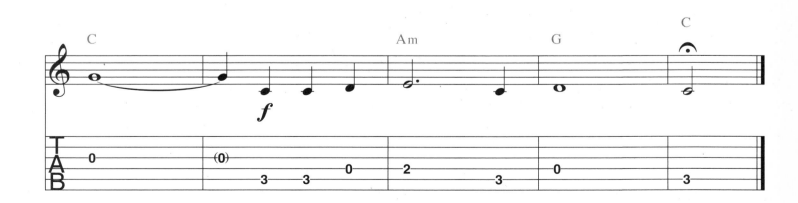

VIDEO EXAMPLE

MORE BASS-CHORD ACCOMPANIMENTS

When you're in $\frac{3}{4}$ time, the bass-chord-chord accompaniment works great. The bass note is the lowest note in the chord and often the note that gives the chord its name (C for the C chord, G for the G or G⁷ chords, etc.). First, play the bass note alone, then play the rest of the chord on the second and third beats.

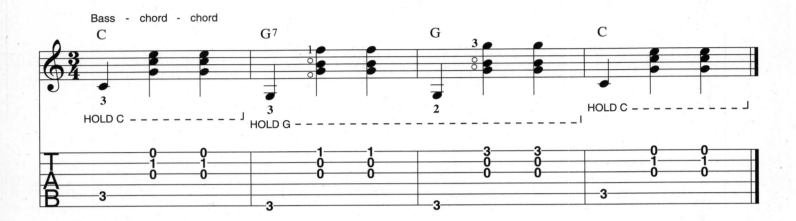

To change things around a bit, you can use another note of the chord as an *alternate bass note,* abbreviated "Alt."

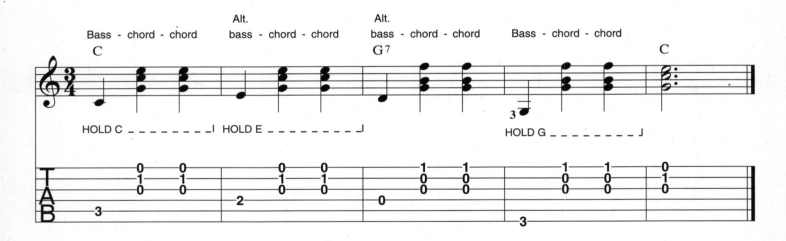

Cielito Lindo

Using the patterns you have learned, play chord accompaniments (using bass and alternate bass notes) to this famous Mexican folk song. Then learn the melody as a guitar solo.

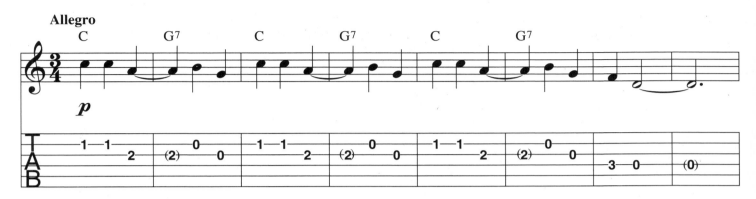

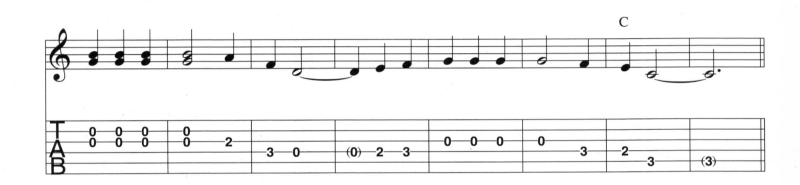

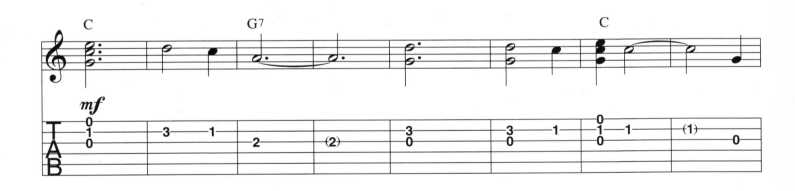

62

EIGHTH NOTES

Eighth notes are black notes that have a flag added to the stem: ♪ or ♫.

Two or more eighth notes are written with a *beam*: ♫ or ♫.

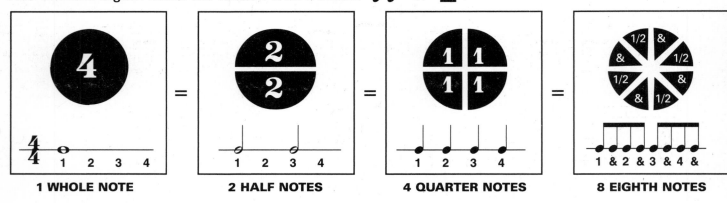

| 1 WHOLE NOTE | 2 HALF NOTES | 4 QUARTER NOTES | 8 EIGHTH NOTES |

Use alternating *downstrokes* ⊓ and *upstrokes* ∨ on eighth notes. This is called *alternate picking*.

COUNT: 1 & 2 & 3 & 4 & 1 & 2 & 3 & 4 &

Jammin' with Eighth Notes

Allegro moderato*

* Moderately fast.

Walkin' with Eighths

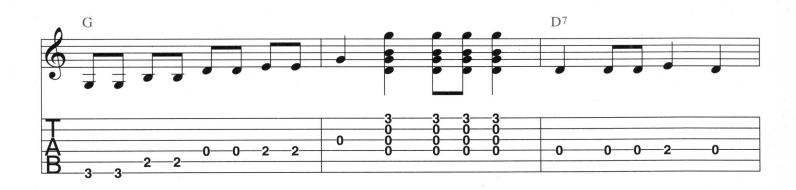

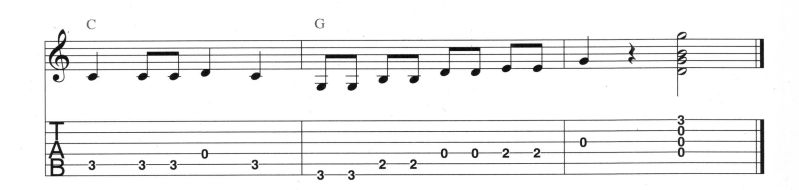

CRESCENDO & DIMINUENDO

Crescendo

Both this sign ◁━━━━━━ and the word *crescendo* mean to get gradually louder.

Diminuendo

Both this sign ━━━━▷ and the word *diminuendo* mean to get gradually softer.

Pachelbel's Canon

Composer Johann Pachelbel lived from 1653 to 1706. Play this piece as a round, like "Row, Row, Row Your Boat." The first player plays the music as written; the second player begins when the first player gets to A.

Pachelbel

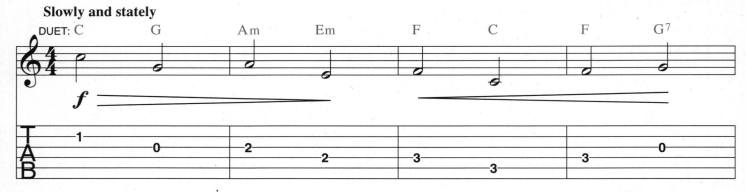

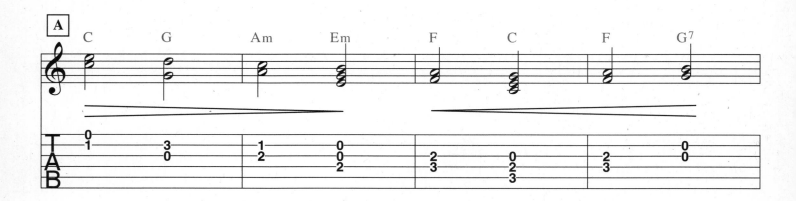

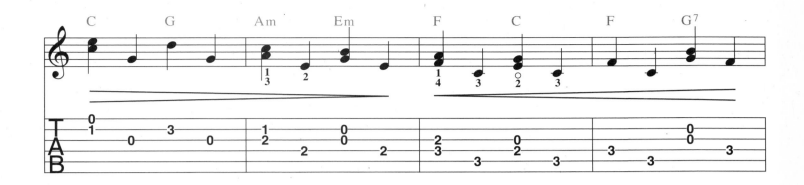

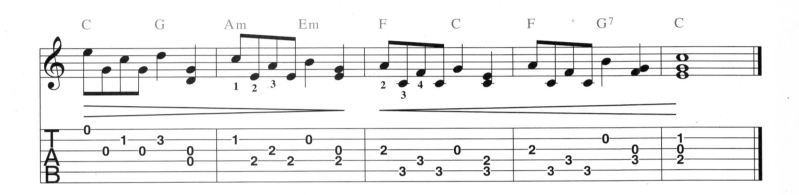

Photo: Cesar Vera, courtesy MCA

DID YOU KNOW?

Blues legend B. B. King has been making his guitar, "Lucille," sing for many years, moving generations of fans with his soulful, heartfelt music. Since the launch of his professional career in the 1950s, his desire to improve the status and acceptability of the blues has set him apart from other players, and he is now commonly referred to as the "greatest living blues guitarist."

VIDEO EXAMPLE

SHARPS ♯, FLATS ♭, AND NATURALS ♮

The distance from one fret to the next fret, up or down, is a *half step*.
Two half steps make a *whole step*.

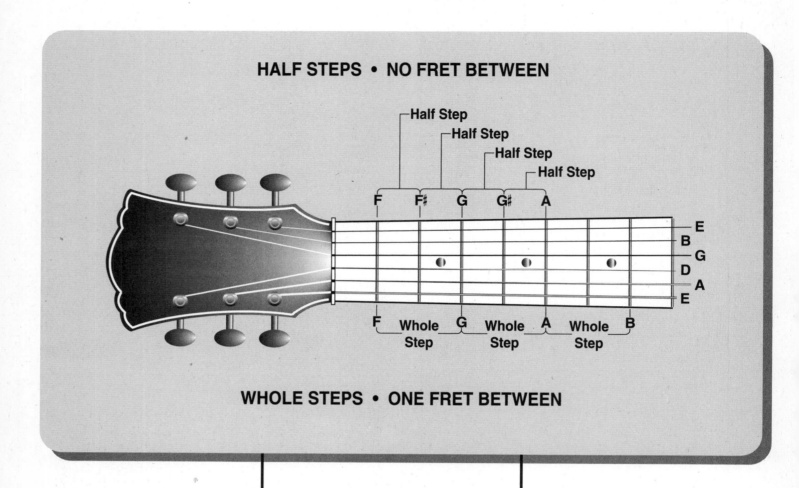

HALF STEPS • NO FRET BETWEEN

WHOLE STEPS • ONE FRET BETWEEN

A *sharp* **raises** a note a half step. Play the next fret higher.

A *flat* **lowers** a note a half step. If the note is fingered, play the next fret lower. If the note is open, play the 4th fret of the next lower string, unless that string is G (3rd string)—then play the 3rd fret.

A *natural* **cancels** a previous sharp or flat. A note that is sharp or flat continues to be sharp or flat throughout the same measure unless it is cancelled by a natural. Flats and sharps only last to the end of the measure.

THE CHROMATIC SCALE

The *chromatic scale* is completely made up of half steps. When the chromatic scale is ascending, it is written with sharps; when it is descending, it is written with flats.

Ascending Chromatic Scale

Descending Chromatic Scale

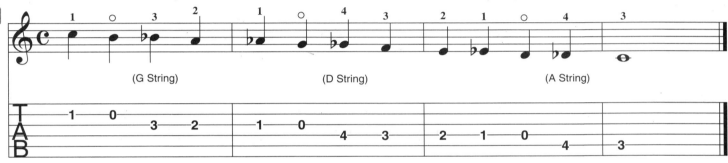

(G String)   (D String)   (A String)

Photo: © Ken Settle

DID YOU KNOW?

Bonnie Raitt writes and performs music deeply rooted in the American classics of country, blues, and rock. Her style features earthy vocals and superb slide guitar playing, and she has amassed a loyal following since the 1980s.

Chromatic Rock

Allegro moderato

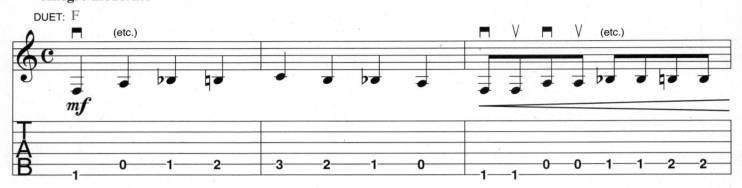

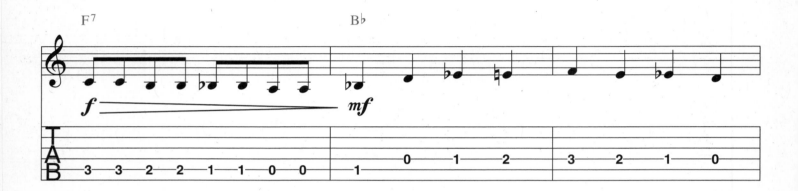

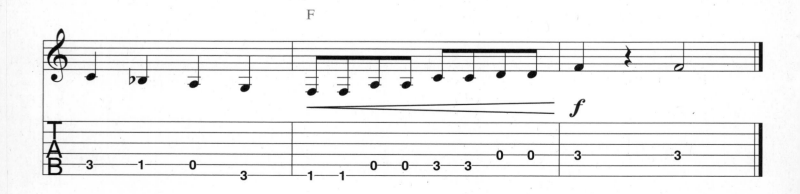

VIDEO EXAMPLE

FOUR-STRING D⁷ CHORD

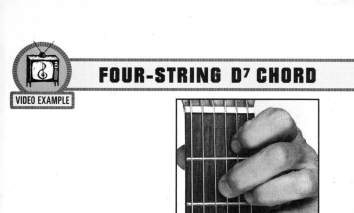

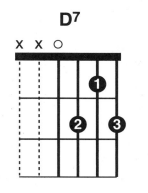

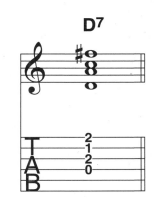

AUDIO EXAMPLE

Blues in G

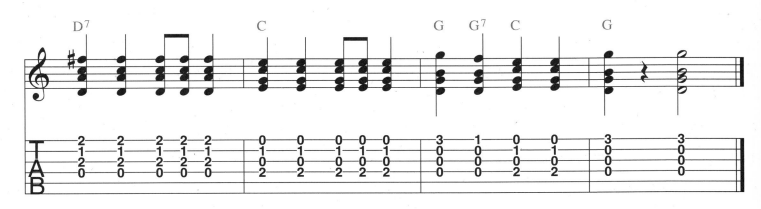

Amazing Grace

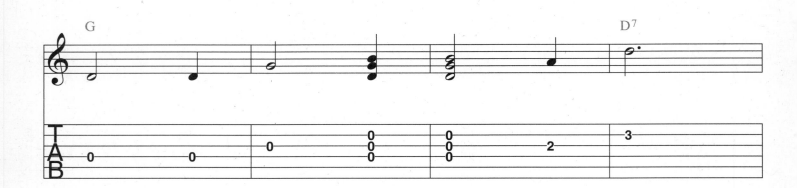

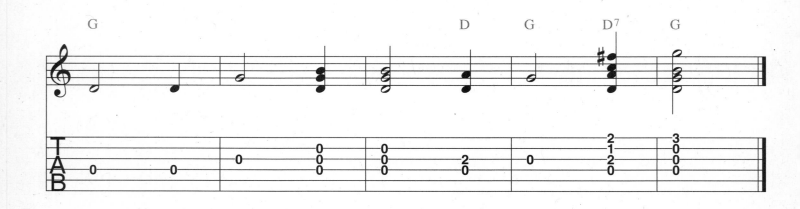

Rockin' the Bach

Adapted from a minuet by J.S. Bach

Moderato

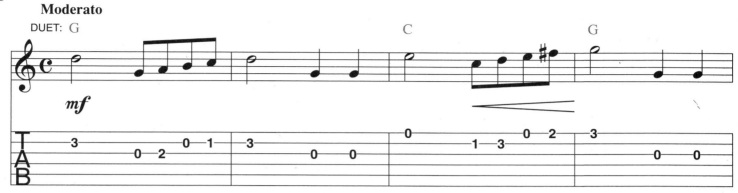

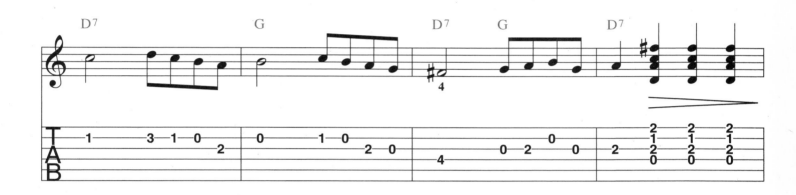

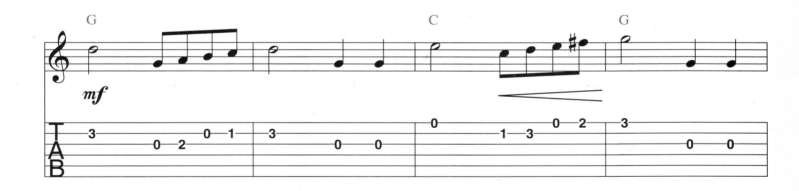

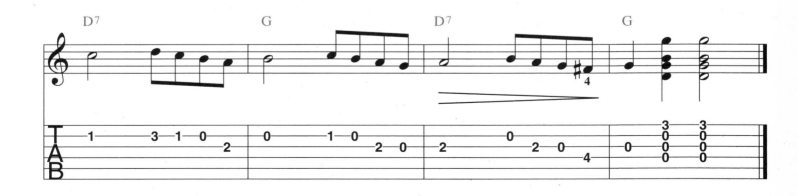

Rockin' Up 'n' Down

DUET: G

THE MAJOR SCALE

A *major scale* is a succession of eight tones in alphabetical order.
All major scales are built using the same pattern:

WHOLE STEP, WHOLE STEP, HALF STEP, WHOLE STEP, WHOLE STEP, WHOLE STEP, HALF STEP

The major scale has eight notes. The highest note, having the same letter-name as the first note, is called the *octave note*.

C Major Scale

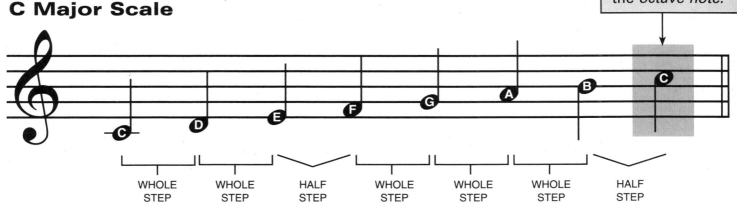

It is easier to visualize whole steps and half steps on a piano keyboard. Notice there is a whole step between all natural notes except from E to F, and B to C.

Whole steps = One key between
Half steps = No key between

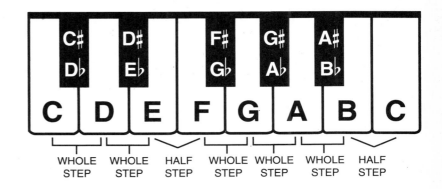

A major scale may be built starting on **any note**, whether natural, sharp or flat.
Using this pattern, write a major scale starting on G.

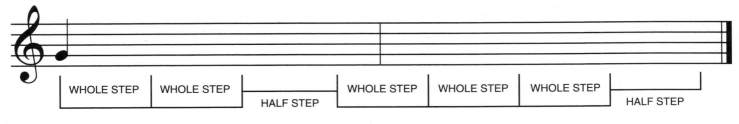

Write a major scale starting on F.

Check: Are the notes in alphabetical order?

VIDEO EXAMPLE

KEY SIGNATURES

The Key of C Major

A piece based on the C major scale is in the *key of C major*.
There are no sharps or flats in the C major scale.

The Key of G Major

A piece based on the G major scale is in the *key of G major*. Since F is sharp in the G scale, every F will be sharp in the key of G major. Instead of writing all the F-sharps in the piece, the sharp is indicated at the beginning, in the *key signature*. Sharps or flats shown in the key signature are effective throughout the piece.

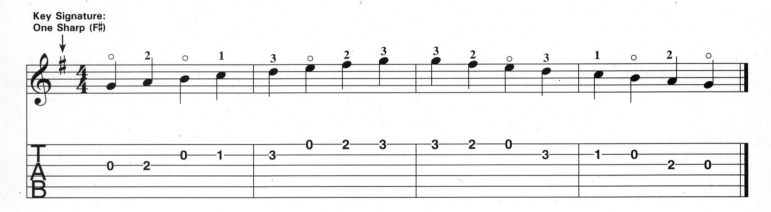

The Key of F Major

A piece based on the F major scale is in the *key of F major*.

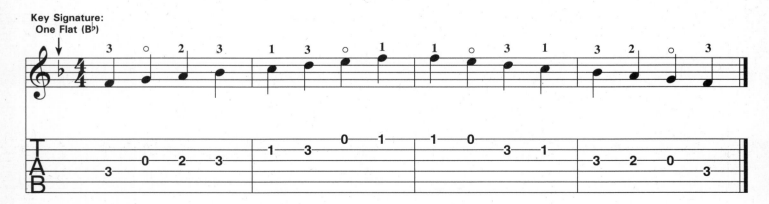

GIVE IT A TRY

You should practice the three scales above every day. If you do this, you will not have any difficulty playing music written in C major, G major or F major.

EIGHTH RESTS

This is an EIGHTH REST.
It means REST for the value of an EIGHTH NOTE.

When eighth notes appear singly, they look like this: ♪ or ♪ .

Single eighth notes are often used with eighth rests: ♪ ⁊ .
COUNT: "1   &"
or: "two - 8ths"

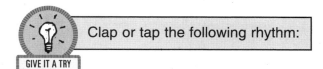

COUNT: 1   &   2   &   3   &   4   &

When an eighth rest follows a fingered note, the sound is cut off by releasing the pressure of the finger on the string. When following an open note, the sound is cut off by touching the string with either a left-hand finger or the heel of the right hand.

Eighth Rest Example #1

Eighth Rest Example #2

Eighth rests may also appear on downbeats. Try to keep an even beat by tapping your foot or silently counting each eighth.

COUNT: 1 & 2 & 3 & 4 &   (etc.)

Eighth Rest Example #3

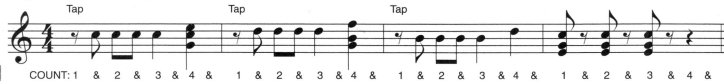

COUNT: 1 & 2 & 3 & 4 &   1 & 2 & 3 & 4 &   1 & 2 & 3 & 4 &   1 & 2 & 3 & 4 &

La Bamba

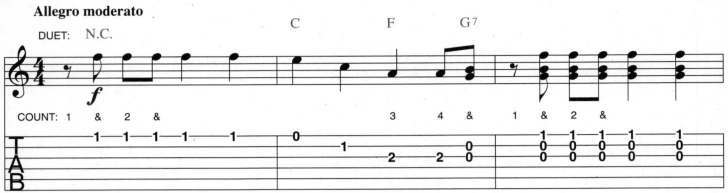

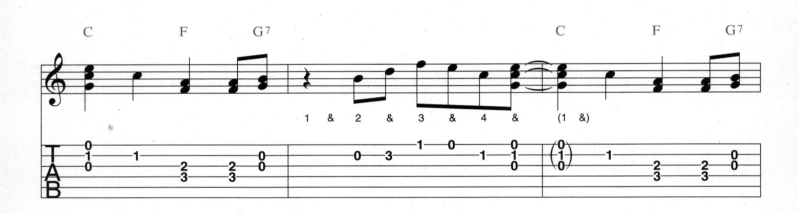

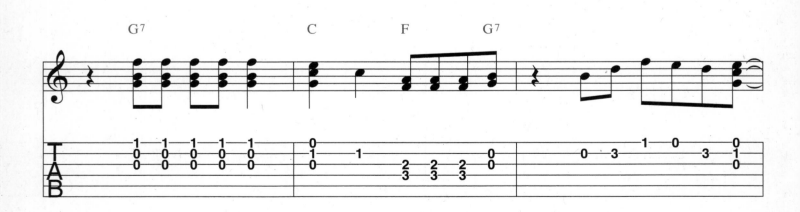

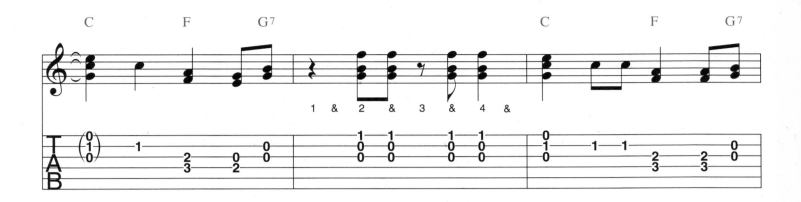

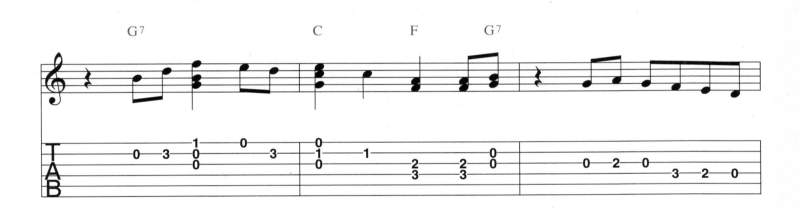

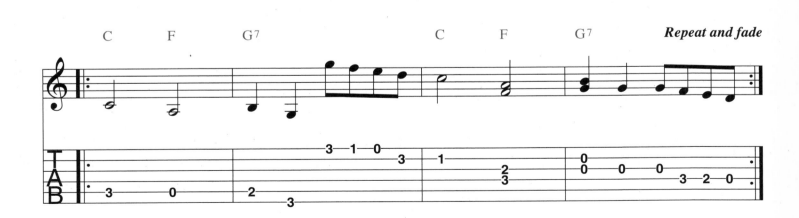

2/4 TIME SIGNATURE

This piece is in 2/4 time, which means there are two beats in each measure.

Accidentals

If sharps, flats or naturals not shown in the key signature occur in the piece, they are called *accidentals.* Accidentals only last through the measure in which they appear.

Bill Bailey

H. Cannon

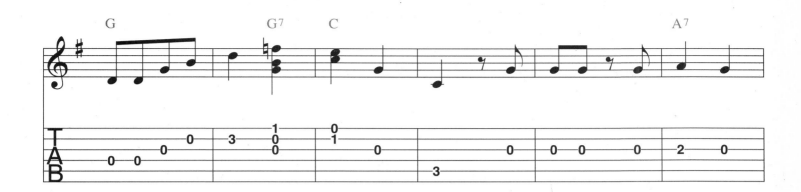

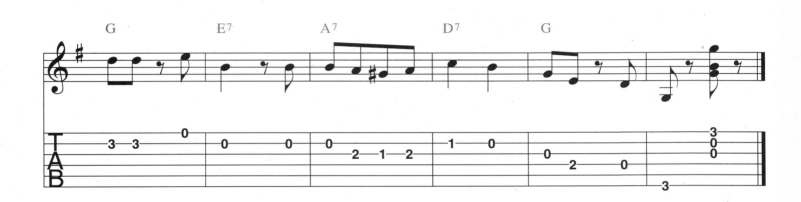

Photo: Ethan Russel, courtesy MCA

The Who took a larger-than-life approach to rock performance, inspired by the theatrical, powerful compositions of guitarist Pete Townshend. Included among these works is rock's first opera, "Tommy," which was released in 1969.

VIDEO EXAMPLE

DOTTED QUARTER NOTES

A DOT INCREASES

THE LENGTH OF A NOTE

BY ONE-HALF!

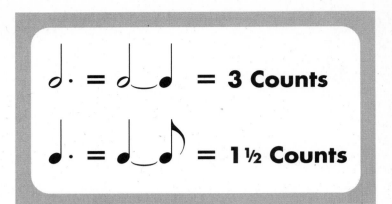

Preparatory Drill

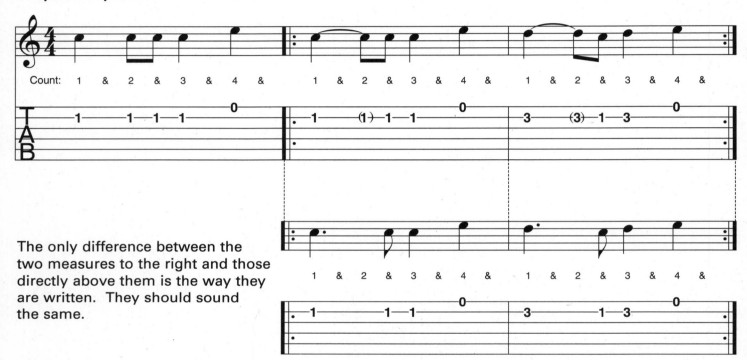

The only difference between the two measures to the right and those directly above them is the way they are written. They should sound the same.

AUDIO EXAMPLE

Auld Lang Syne

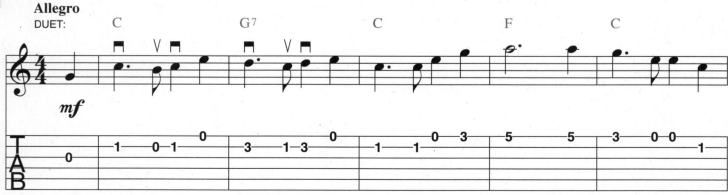

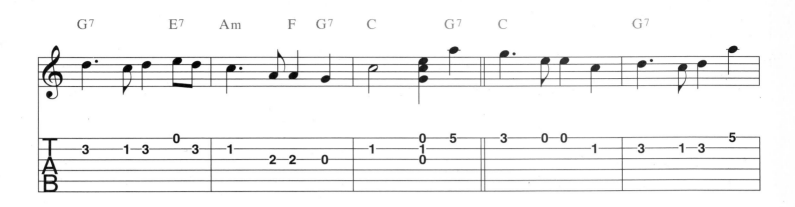

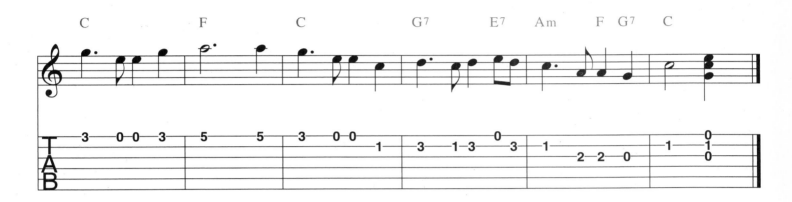

DID YOU KNOW?

Brian May received his first guitar on his 7th birthday, and the world of rock is grateful. His guitar playing and vocals contributed to the unique sound of the highly successful group Queen starting in the early 1970s. May was also a successful songwriter, having penned Queen's hit song "We Will Rock You."

Photo: © Ken Settle

Hava Nagila

Israeli folk song

Brightly

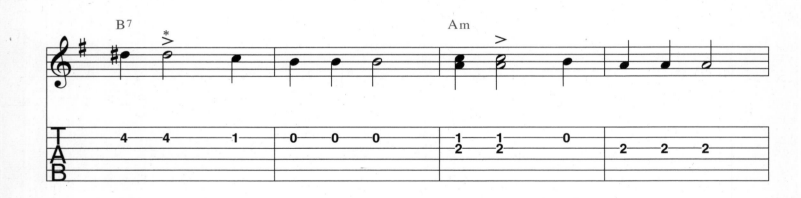

* > = Accent. Play the note a little louder.

KEY OF C MAJOR

C Major Scale

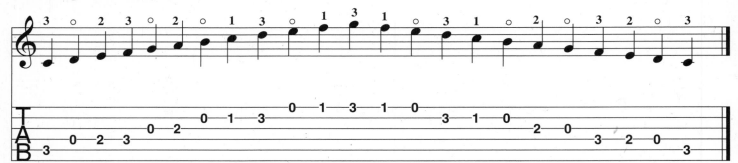

Three Chords in C Major

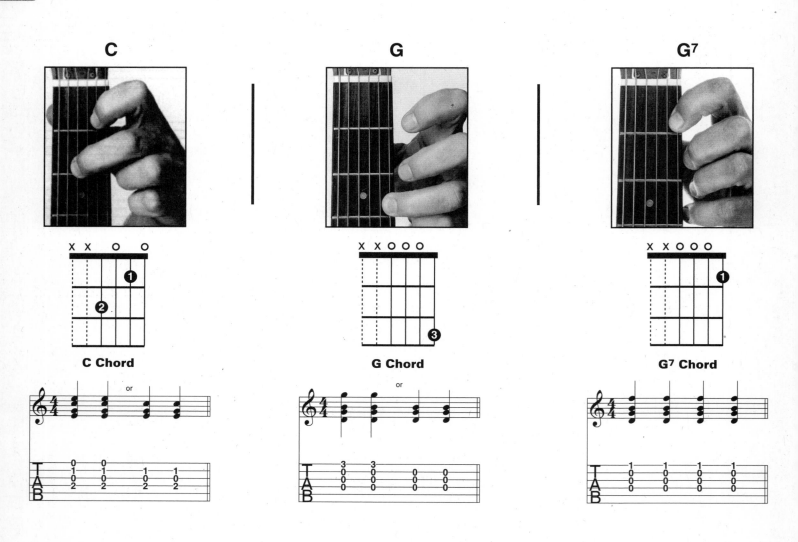

C

C Chord

G

G Chord

G⁷

G⁷ Chord

Accompaniment in C Major

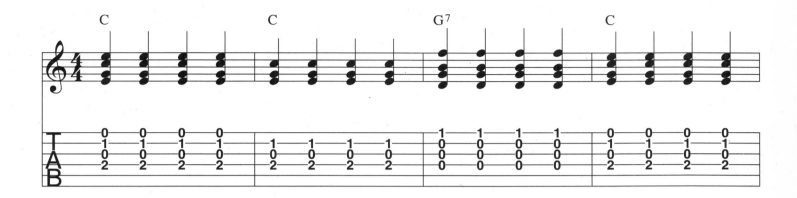

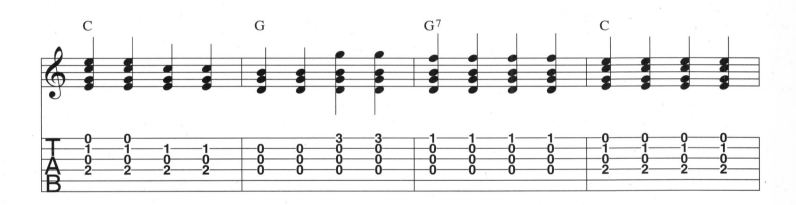

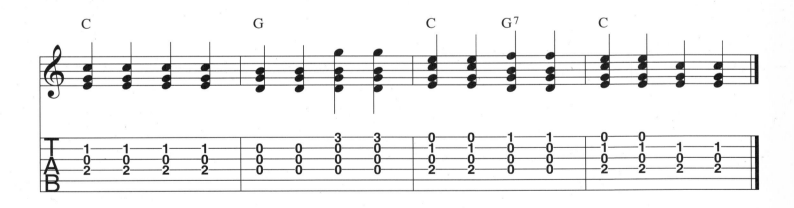

TWO-OCTAVE C MAJOR SCALE

The C major scale can be extended to a full two octaves by adding high A, high B and high C.

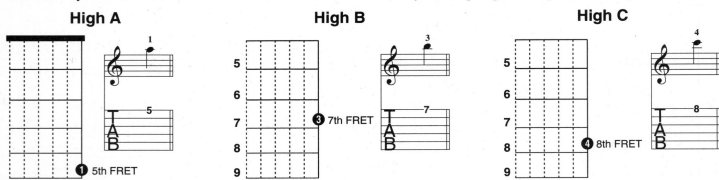

Ascending Two-Octave C Major Scale

Shift the hand up the neck

Descending Two-Octave C Major Scale

Shift down the neck

Practice these scales every day. Make every effort to play the notes under the brackets as smoothly as possible.

AUDIO EXAMPLE

Joy to the World

Handel

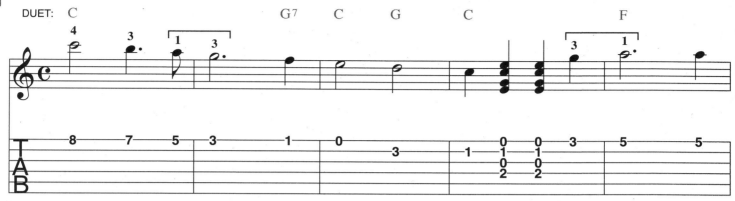

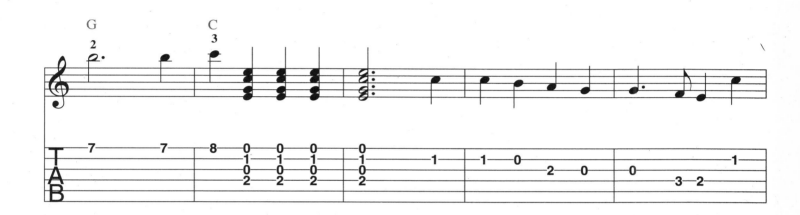

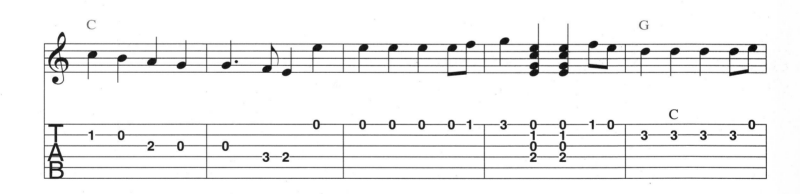

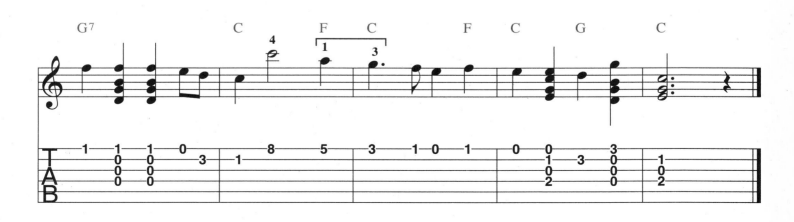

THREE-STRING F MINOR CHORD

The F minor chord is a new chord that requires putting your first
finger across three strings. Press hard near (but not on) the 1st fret.

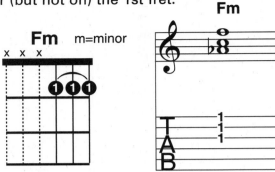

Home on the Range

American cowboy song

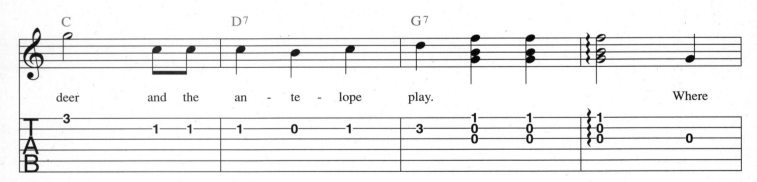

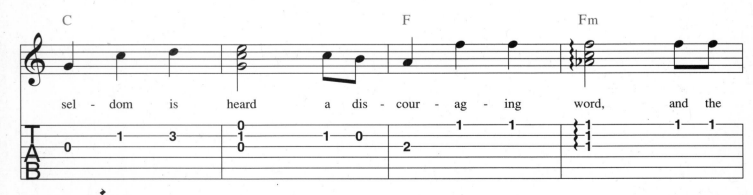

* A wavy line in front of a chord means to run the pick across the strings more slowly to obtain a rippling, harp-like sound. The
technical term for creating this effect is the Italian word *arpeggiando*, often abbreviated "arp."

Variation on Little Brown Jug

This tune will help you develop your technique for playing repeated notes. Pay attention to the picking directions.

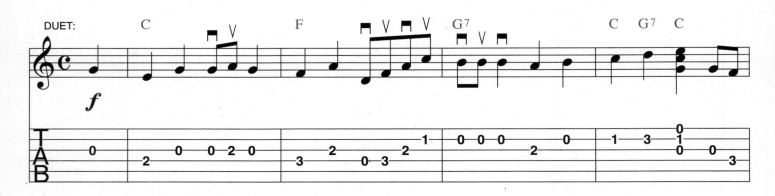

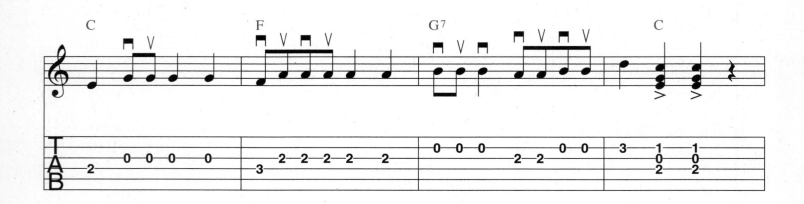

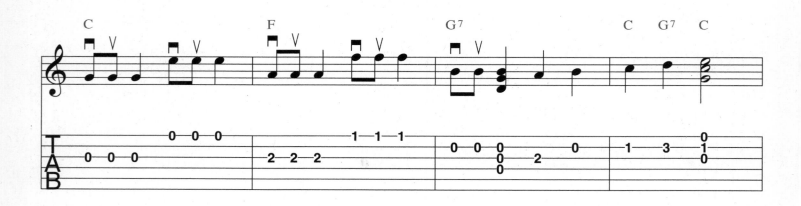

Performer and songwriter Woody Guthrie is an American folk hero. A series of hardships among his early family experiences lead to life-long sympathies for the poor and downtrodden that were frequently expressed in his music. Guthrie started playing guitar in 1926, but didn't realize a life as a performer until 1938 when he hosted a radio show. He eventually went on to record albums and wrote many popular folk songs including "This Land Is Your Land."

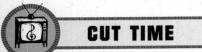

CUT TIME

This symbol **¢** stands for *cut time,* which means the time values of the notes are cut in half. The half note receives one beat, and the quarter note receives one-half beat.

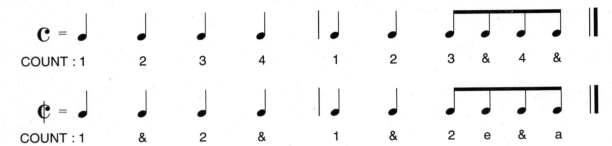

Variation on Jim Crack Corn

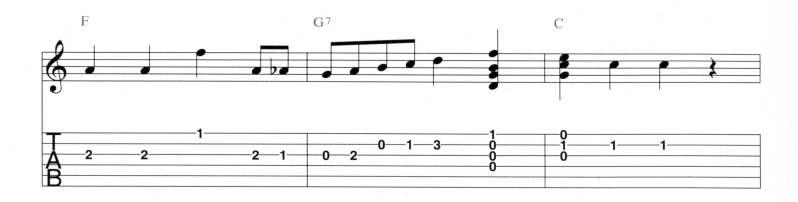

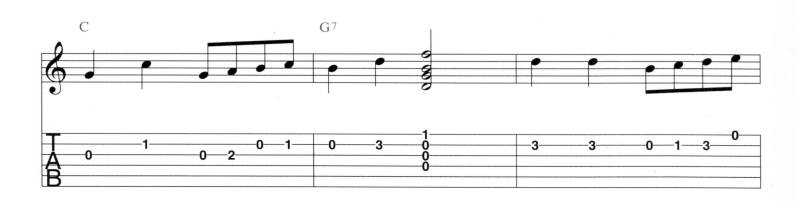

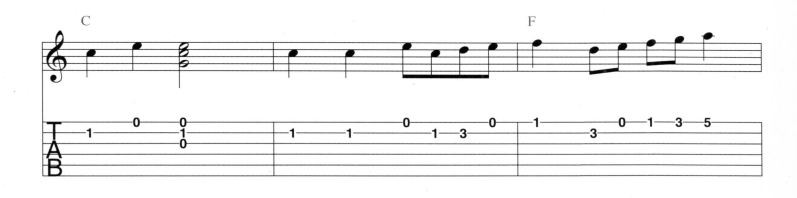

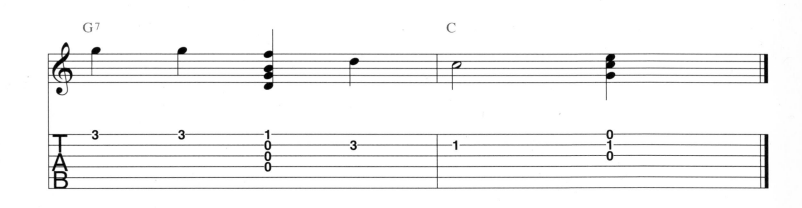

KEY OF G MAJOR

As you learned on page 74, the key signature of one sharp indicates the key of G major. All F's are played as F-sharp unless otherwise indicated by a natural sign.

AUDIO EXAMPLE

G Major Scale

VIDEO EXAMPLE

The Three Principal Chords in G Major

The three principal (most commonly used) chords in any key are built on the first, fourth and fifth notes of the scale. The chord built on the fifth note usually adds a seventh tone to it. The chords are known as 1, 4, 5$^{(7)}$ chords and are sometimes indicated by Roman numerals: I, IV, V^7. The three principal chords in the key of G major are G, C and D^7.

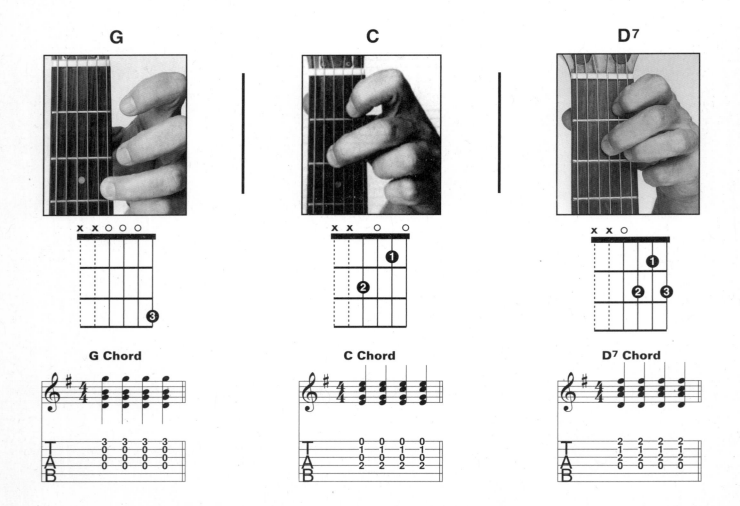

Tiritomba

First, learn the melody of this song. It's in the key of G and makes use of many repeated notes. Then, play along with the DVD or have your teacher or a friend play the melody while you strum the chords, four to each measure.

Shortnin' Bread

This tune will help you develop your technique for playing skips.

KEY OF A MINOR

For every major key there is a minor key called the *relative minor* that has the same key signature. The keys of A minor and C major are relative keys because they have the same key signature (no sharps, no flats). The relative minor scale is built on the sixth tone of the major scale. Chords are built on the harmonic minor scale, which has its seventh step *augmented* (raised a half step).

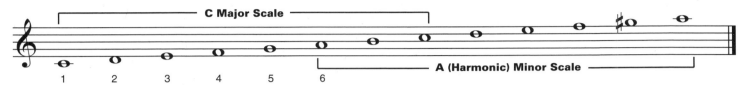

Two-Octave A Harmonic Minor Scale

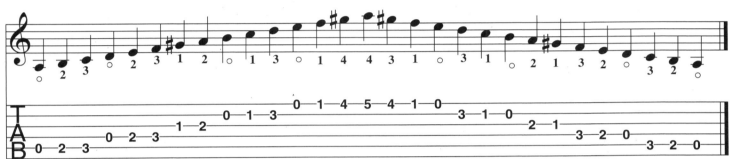

The Three Principal Chords in A Minor

Am

Dm

E⁷

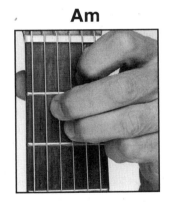

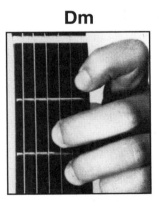

Five-String Am Chord

Four-String Dm Chord

Six-String E⁷ Chord

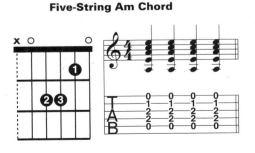

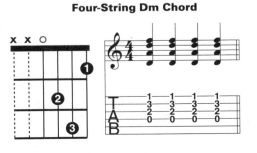

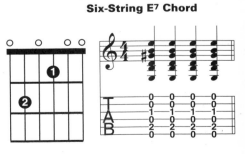

AUDIO EXAMPLE

Accompaniments in A Minor

The slash / means to play the indicated chord or to repeat the previous chord.

A Minor Accompaniment #1

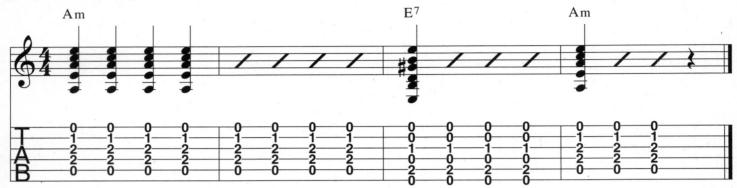

A Minor Accompaniment #2

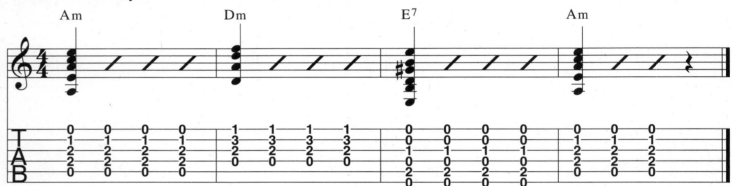

A Minor Accompaniment #3

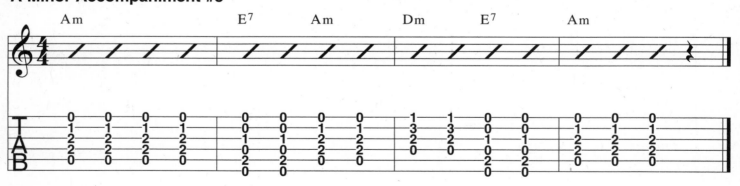

FOUR-STRING F CHORD

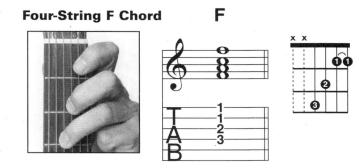

Four-String F Chord

Bass-Chord Accompaniment in the Key of C Major

The three principal chords in the key of C major are C, F and G^7. Chord accompaniment is considerably improved by replacing the first chord of each measure with a bass note. The simplest bass note is the *root* (the letter-name) of the chord.

With the C (I) chord, play the bass note C.

With the F (IV) chord, play the bass note F.

With the G or G^7 (V^7) chord, play the bass note G.

* Some guitarists use the left thumb to finger bass notes on the low E string when followed by a chord. You can also try this technique. Use whichever is most comfortable for you.

The Entertainer

Joplin

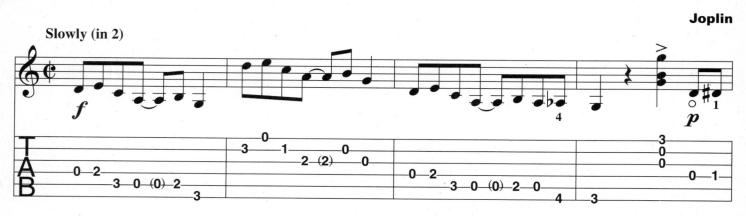

PART 2: ROCK GUITAR

In this section of the book, you'll use the skills and knowledge you have gained so far and put them together with some important new concepts and techniques to start playing rock! You'll learn new chords, scales, rhythms and even techniques like bending and slides. Also, you will learn how to solo using the pentatonic scale and the blues scale. There are some great jam tracks to practice with, and licks in the styles of the masters. Now, let's get started with some new chords.

ROCKIN' WITH CHORDS

Here are some new chords to expand your vocabulary and help you move into playing rock and blues styles.

The Six-String E Chord

Strum downwards across all six strings. Experiment with the sound of this chord playing all down strokes. Play it loud. Play it soft. Play it all levels in between. This is the chord that launched a thousand rock hits. Learn it well and it will be your friend for life.

Two examples of great uses for an E chord are: the opening of The Who's "I Can See For Miles" or John Mellencamp's "Rockin' in the USA."

E

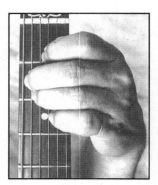

The Four-String D Chord

This chord requires a little more finesse to play, since you only play the top four strings (E-1st, B-2nd, G-3rd, D-4th). The open low E (6th) string does not fit this chord, and while the A works, it is better to have the D string at the bottom of the D chord, since D is the root of the chord. Try the chord with the low E string included. You'll hear that it doesn't sound right.

D

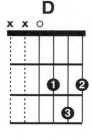

Rhythmic Notation

Rhythmic notation is a way of communicating the sequence of chords that make up a song without standard music notation or TAB. This sequence of chords is called the *progression*. Think of it as a road map down the musical highway. It tells you what chord is coming next, when to repeat a section, when to go on to a new section, and so on. The three principle chords you learned earlier for different keys were progressions.

Rhythmic notation is written on a staff, but with a different style of note head. For now, we will use rhythmic notation on a simple time line. Use the chord names above the staff to determine which chords to play.

Here are the symbols you need to know:

◇ = Whole note. Strum the chord and hold it for four beats.

◇ = Half note. Strum the chord and hold it for two beats.

◗ = Quarter note. Strum the chord and hold it for one beat.

One slash or diamond equals one chord stoke. It's that simple. Read from left to right, just like reading words on a page.

Now let's try playing the E chord and then the D chord, one after the other, following the rhythmic notation. Do it 10 to 15 times. Start slowly. Then, speed it up a little, and you have the chords for songs like "Tequila" by the Champs or "Break On Through" by The Doors.

Dig in the Chords

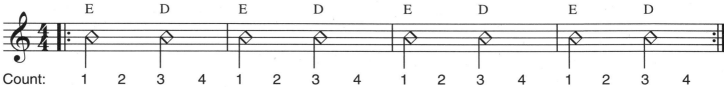

Count: 1   2   3   4   1   2   3   4   1   2   3   4   1   2   3   4

The Five-String A Chord

The next chord is the five-string A Major chord.

The five-string A Major chord poses another challenge since you have to press your 1st, 2nd and 3rd fingers of the left hand in a row on the second fret of the D (4th), G (3rd) and B (2nd) strings. Be patient and work at it. This is a great chord, and once learned, is a perfect match for the E and D chords.

Let's try putting all three chords together in a progression that is similar to the classic song "Gloria" by Van Morrison.

As your left-hand fingers are moving from chord to chord, don't neglect your right-hand picking. "Talking 'Bout My Baby #1" is easy since all the strokes are downstrokes.

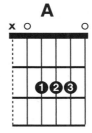

Talking 'Bout My Baby #1

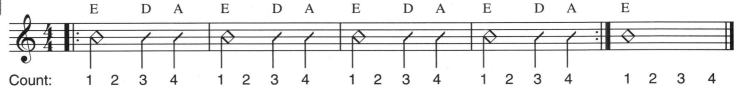

Count: 1   2   3   4   1   2   3   4   1   2   3   4   1   2   3   4   1   2   3   4

Lots of people have difficulty changing chords when they are learning new, more complicated chords. It is not easy to change all three fingers in one position to a completely new shape and back in the space of less than a second. Changing from one chord to another takes a lot of practice, and should always be practiced slowly at first.

POWER CHORDS

In a pinch, you can play just the bottom two strings of a chord. These chords are called *5th* or *power chords*. Power chords are indicated with the chord name and the number "5." So, an E power chord would be written "E5." If you crank up a little distortion on your amp, these chords can really sound full and powerful.

DID YOU KNOW?

Distortion is that aggressive, buzzing sound commonly heard in loud guitar music. It is usually caused by overpowering your speakers with too much amplification (with the amp turned up to 11!). You can also use a distortion pedal, or if there is one, turn on the amp's distortion switch.

TIPS

Playing just the bottom two notes of any chord will make it easier to play and give it a heavy rock sound.

E5

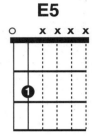

D5

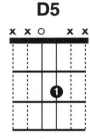

A5

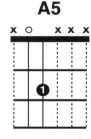

Let's try "Talking 'Bout My Baby" using just the bottom two strings of each chord.

Try different struming patterns, such as ⊓ ⊓ ⊓ ⊓ or ⊓ V ⊓ V.

AUDIO EXAMPLE

Two-String Talking 'Bout My Baby

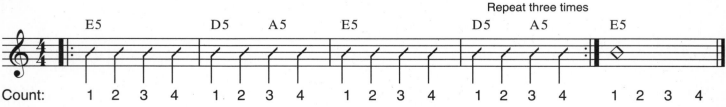

The Five-String C Chord

The next tune uses a five-string C chord as well as the chords we've already learned. Here is the diagram for the C chord:

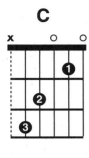

Here's a simple song written in just rhythmic notation:

Four-Chord Rock

Review the chords on page 104. Remember how fat and powerful they sounded with a bit of distortion on them? You can take those simple chords and move them up and down the neck to make dozens of new power chords. All of these chords involve only two strings, either the 6th and 5th, or the 5th and 4th.

6th-String-Root Power Chords

The trick here is to move the E5 chord form you learned on page 104 to another root. Remember, the root is the note that gives the chord its name. E is the root of the E5 chord. This low E is on the 6th string. If you move up one fret, using your 1st finger to replace the open string, you have the F5 chord, because F is the 1st fret of the 6th string. Move it up one more fret and you have the F♯5 chord. Move it up yet another fret and you have the G5 chord.

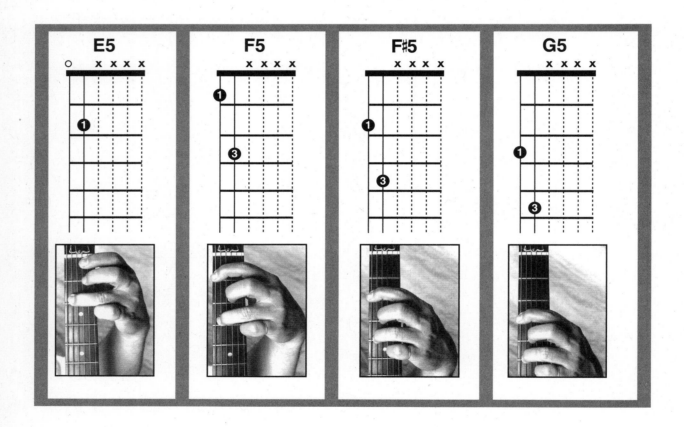

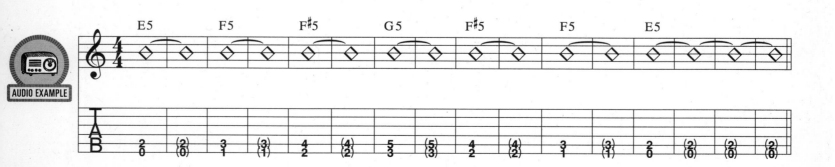

5th-String-Root Power Chords

The same idea behind 6th string power chords applies to 5th string power chords. The only difference is that the roots are now on the 5th string.

Move the A5 chord (including the root) up one fret, and you have the B♭5. Move it up one more fret and you have the B5 chord. Move it up one more fret and you have the C5 chord.

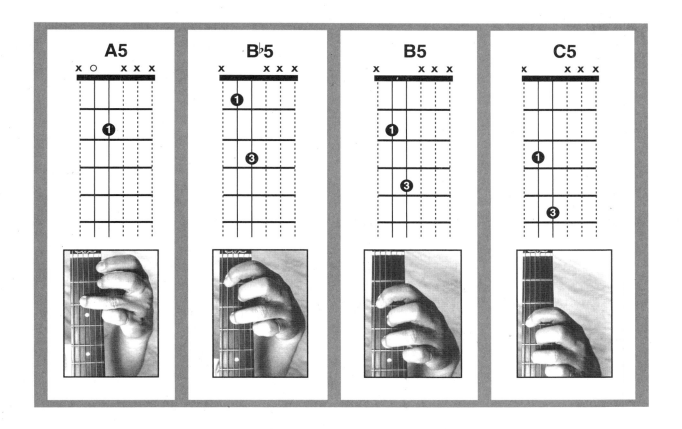

Let's try the same exercise that we did on page 106 but this time on the A string.

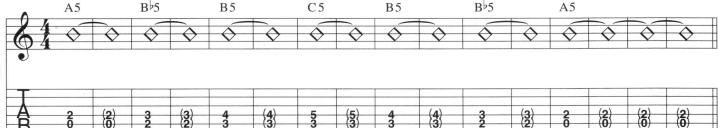

D. C. AL FINE AND FORM

D. C. al Fine stands for *Da Capo al Fine*, an Italian phrase meaning to return to the beginning and play to the "Fine" or end. Often, the "Fine" will appear somewhere other than the last measure. Generally, repeats are ignored during the Da Capo. Notice that the first section is marked A, and is repeated. The second section is marked B. Musicians often refer to the sections of a song this way. The *form* (order of musical events) of this song can be expressed this way:

A A B A B

Now lets put both 6th-string-root and 5th-string-root power chords together in a song.

Shakin' the Rafters

Medium Fast

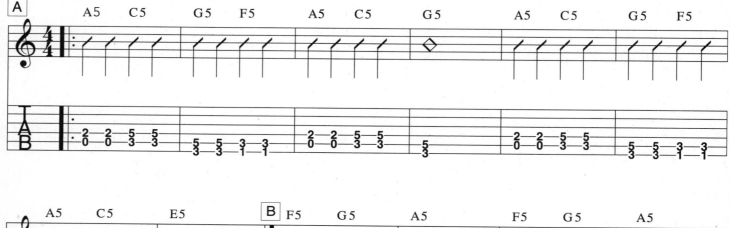

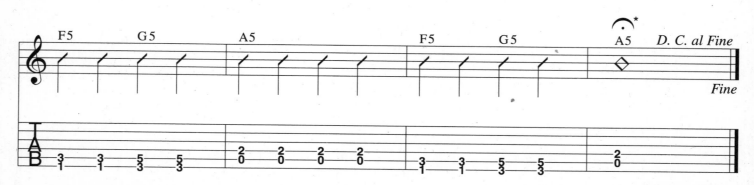

* Last time only

EIGHTH NOTES IN RYTHMIC NOTATION

In rhythmic notation, eighth notes look like quarter notes that have a flag added to the stem:

Two or more eighth notes are written with a beam:

As you learned on page 62, it is helpful to count eighth notes "1 & 2 & 3 & 4 &." The next song will give you some practice reading eighth notes in rhythmic notation.

Below is the form of "Lead and Alchemy." Notice there are three sections: [A], [B] and [C].

[A][A][A][B][B][A][A][B][B][A][C]

The [C] section is the *Coda*, which is an ending section.

Lead and Alchemy

Slow Metallic Rock

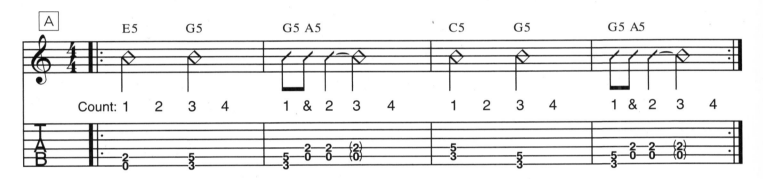

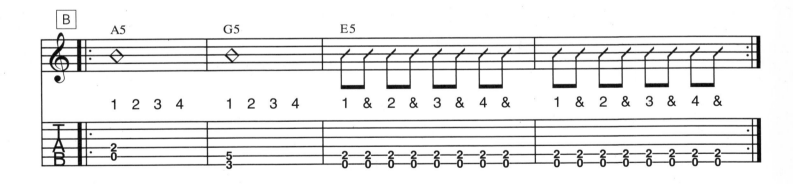

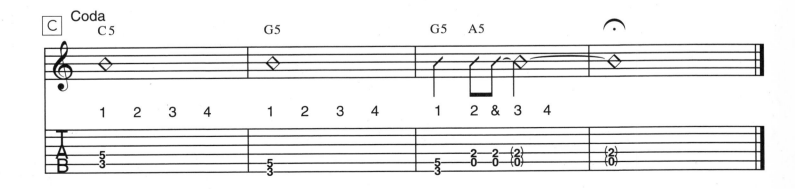

MOVABLE CHORDS OR BARRE CHORDS

Once you've mastered the open chords and power chords found earlier in this book, it's time to learn these movable chords. They are also called *barre chords*. A barre chord is played by laying your 1st finger on its left side across more than one string. You will need to apply some extra pressure, and hold your finger as straight as you can to make sure that every note in the barre rings clearly. It is helpful to bring your left elbow in closer to your side. You already learned a barre chord on page 88 (F minor).

Since barre chords contain no open strings, you can then move them all around the neck. There are several kinds of barre chords. The most common are those based on an E major chord and those based on an A major chord.

E-Major-Shape Barre Chords

Play an E major chord, but use your 3rd, 4th and 2nd fingers, keeping your 1st finger free to barre. Now move these fingers up one fret, and lay your 1st finger across all six strings at the 1st fret. Now, your 1st finger is holding the lowest and top two strings in the chord, replacing the open strings. The note on the 6th string is the root in this kind of barre chord, so whatever note the 1st finger is holding on the 6th string names the root of the chord. For instance, the barre chord on the 1st fret is an F major chord, because the 1st fret on the 6th string is an F.

E   F

Observe how knowing the names of the notes on the 6th string lets you use one chord shape to play four different chords:

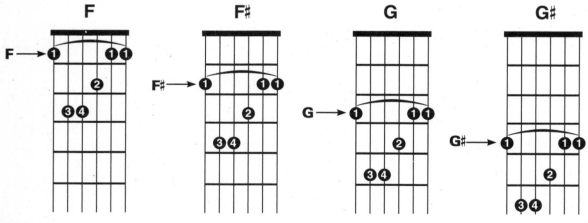

F   F#   G   G#

E-Shape Barre Exercise

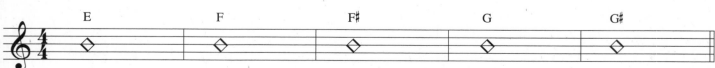

It can be little tricky pushing down all six strings and getting a clear sound with barre chords, but with adequate practice on them you can open up worlds of musical possibilities.

A-Major-Shape Barre Chords

In the same manner that you created barre chords using the E Major chord shape, you can create barre chords using the A Major chord shape. Play the A chord, but instead of using the 1st, 2nd and 3rd fingers, play all three notes with a 3rd finger barre. In other words, lay your 3rd finger down across all three notes. Don't worry—your 1st string isn't necessary for the barre chord, so you don't have to strain yourself to clear it with your 3rd finger. In fact, your 3rd finger should bump into the 1st string, muting it. Now, move this shape up one fret, laying your 1st finger down across the top five strings, replacing the open strings with a barre.

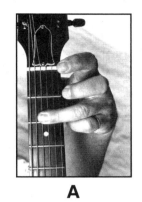

A

B♭

In A Major shape barre chords, the roots of the chords are all on the 5th string, so whatever note the 1st finger is holding on the 5th string names the root of the chord. For instance, this barre chord on the 1st fret is a B♭ major chord, because the 1st fret on the 5th string is a B♭.

Observe how knowing the names of the notes on the 5th string lets you use one chord shape to play four different chords:

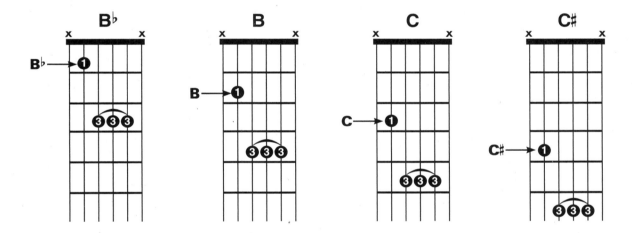

AUDIO EXAMPLE

A-Shape Barre Exercise

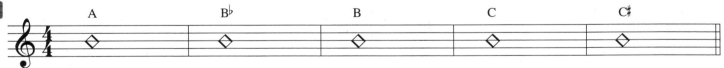

You Got Me Rockin'

Medium Fast

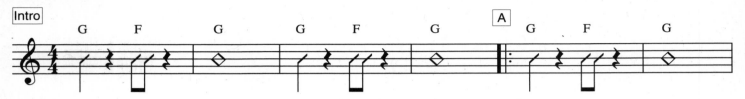

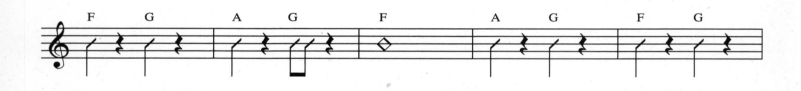

Comin' Around

The rhythm guitar style in this tune is similar to the one in the Green Day song, "When I Come Around." It is essentially a chord pattern containing single note lines which together make up a unified part. The [A] section is repeated ten times during the first chorus, and then nine times on choruses two through five. The [A] section during the last chorus repeats four times before going to the last two measures.

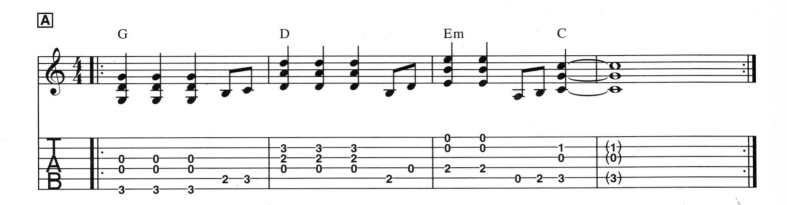

Form
Listen to rhythm part on chorus 1. Play rhythm guitar on choruses 2-3. Solo on chorus 4. Play rhythm on chorus 5.

In this section, the longer examples on the recording are repeated. The second time through the form features the rhythm instruments only. You can use these tracks to practice the solos from this section, and also to practice constructing your own solos using the information presented here. Also note there is a collection of jam tracks for further practice on pages 140–146.

Before moving on, look below and at the following page for brief descriptions of some conventions and basic concepts used in this section.

READING FINGERBOARD SCALE DIAGRAMS

The scales referenced in this book are often presented with suggested fingerings using *fingerboard diagrams*. These diagrams are graphic depictions of the guitar neck and the frets where the notes of a particular scale are played. The horizontal lines represent the strings, with the 1st string (high E) at the top and the 6th string (low E) at the bottom. The vertical lines represent the frets, which are numbered below the diagram. White dots indicate the *tonic* (see page 115) notes of the scale, while black dots are used for the other notes of the scale. The numbers next to the dots indicate which left-hand fingers to use. (The fingers of the left hand are numbered 1–4, starting with the index finger.)

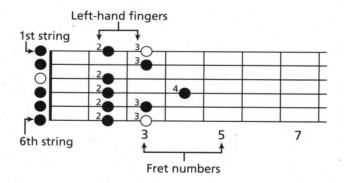

O = Tonic

BASIC CONCEPTS REVIEW

Before you dive into these solos, make sure you know some basic scale and chord theory. The following pages will often refer to the concepts discussed on this page. Some of this is review for you, but it is very important you are comfortable with everything here before continuing.

The Major Scale

As you learned on page 73, the major scale consists of seven notes built using a specific formula of whole steps (two frets) and half steps (one fret). These seven notes are often referred to using scale degrees, or numerals that correspond to the notes' location in a particular scale. The *tonic* (or first note of the scale) is always the note from which a scale derives its name, and will be shown as a white dot in scale diagrams throughout this book (see page 116). The following example shows the C major scale with its scale degrees numbered.

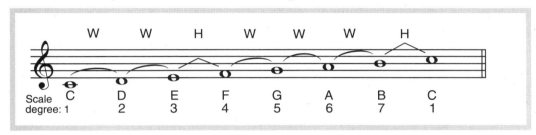

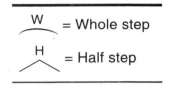

As you encounter other scales in this book, you will notice that they are often compared to the major scale. *Flat* (♭ or one half step lower) and *sharp* (♯ or one half step higher) symbols are used to alter scale degrees as necessary.

Triads and Diatonic Harmony

Once you are familiar with major scale construction, the next step is to build *triads*, or three-note chords, based on each note in the scale. The lowest note, which gives a chord its name, is called the *root*. Triads are constructed by stacking two notes above the root note, each an *interval* of a *diatonic* 3rd apart. An interval is the distance between two pitches. The term diatonic refers to notes or chords that occur naturally within a particular scale or key. You can see the pattern of triads built from a major scale below.

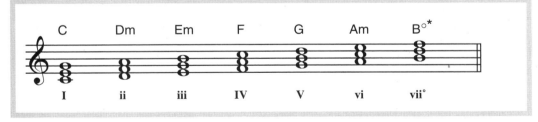

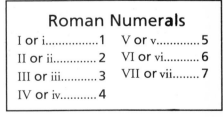

* = Diminished

The examples on these pages will often use Roman numerals to quickly refer to harmonic relationships that can be transferred to any key. The above example shows that uppercase Roman numerals correspond to major triads, while lowercase Roman numerals refer to minor or diminished (○) chords. In some cases, it is also possible for Roman numerals to be modified by flats or sharps for the sake of simplicity.

Now that this technical information is out of the way, get your guitar tuned up and start rockin'!

THE MINOR PENTATONIC SCALE

Let's jump right in and start soloing. One of the most important and popular scales for solos in all styles of rock music is the *minor pentatonic scale*. The minor pentatonic scale is made up of five notes that follow the pattern of scale degrees: 1–♭3–4–5–♭7. The flat (♭) symbol indicates that the interval it modifies is one half step, or one fret, lower in pitch than the corresponding note of the major scale. For example, the second note in this scale is a *minor 3rd* because of the flat. Look at the notation below for a one-octave E minor pentatonic scale. Notice there is no 2 or 6; these scale degrees are omitted in minor pentatonic scales.

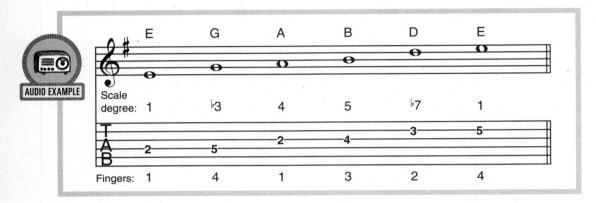

Below are some fingering patterns for the E minor pentatonic scale in various *positions* along the neck. A position on the guitar is a four-fret range that takes its name from the fret on which your 1st finger is located. For example, if you are playing in 2nd position, your 1st finger will play notes on the 2nd fret. Remember that the tonic note of the scale is depicted in these fretboard diagrams with a white dot.

E Minor Pentatonic Scale Fingerings

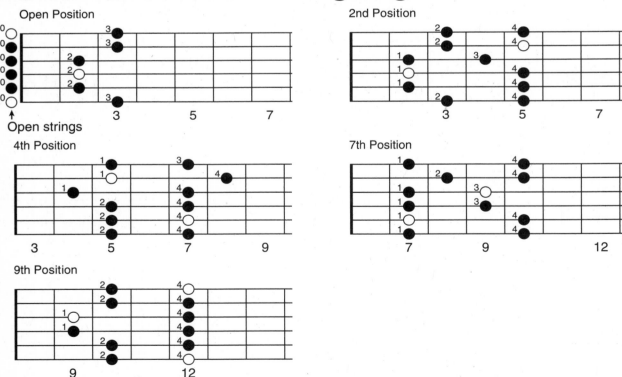

Practice each of these fingerings individually, then try moving from one position to the next to get comfortable playing this scale over the entire fretboard. This scale works well with diatonic minor chords and power chords (pages 106–107) in the key of the scale, and it can even work well with major chords and other progressions, as you will see throughout this section. (Note that some of the solos may require you to use different left-hand fingers than those indicated above; this is to accommodate easier transitions between parts in the solos.)

It is worthwhile to practice the minor pentatonic scale in other keys because it is so popular. Let's get started in the key of A minor with the fingerings below.

A Minor Pentatonic Scale Fingerings

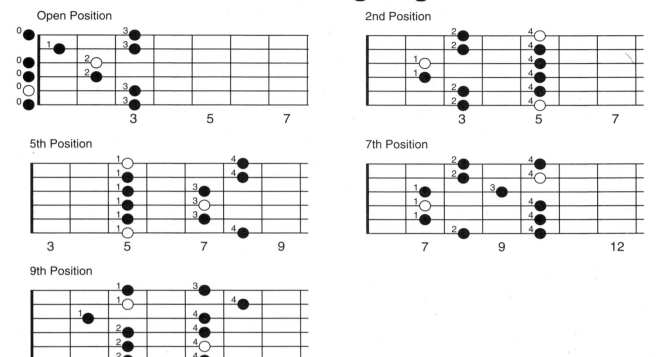

Hammer-Ons and Pull-Offs

GIVE IT A TRY

In the music so far in this book, every note was picked with the right hand. Incorporating other techniques will add more dimension to your solos.

Hammer-ons and *pull-offs* are two important techniques for any guitarist. They are examples of *legato* playing, where the right hand does not pick every note. A hammer-on is when you pick the first note, then "hammer" onto a higher fret on the same string with another finger to sound a second note without picking a second time. A pull-off is just the opposite; you fret a note and, after picking it, pull off to a lower note on the same string. Look at the notation and tablature below.

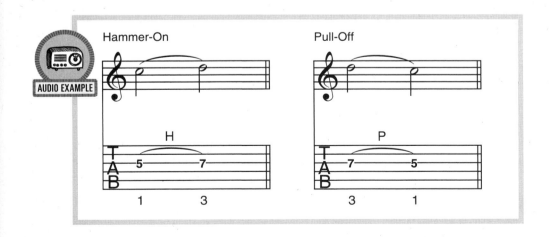

H	
	= Hammer-on
P	
	= Pull-off

THE BLUES SCALE

The *blues scale is* another important scale for rock soloists due to the strong connection between the blues and rock music. Many famous rock musicians are known for using this scale, including Jimi Hendrix, Jimmy Page, Angus Young, Billy Gibbons, and Eric Clapton, among others.

First, let's look at the structure of this scale, which is very similar to the minor pentatonic scale (1–♭3–4–5–♭7), but includes the note a *tritone* above the root. A tritone is another term for an interval of an *augmented 4th* or a *diminished 5th*. Check out the TAB and notation for the G blues scale below to get a better understanding.

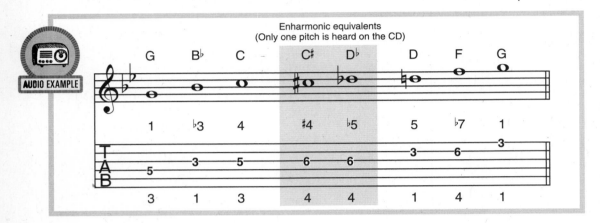

As you can see, C♯ and D♭ are played on the same fret, and are said to be *enharmonic equivalents*; that is, two notes that are notated differently, but share the same pitch. Therefore, the blues scale can be spelled either 1–♭3–4–♯4–5–♭7 or 1–♭3–4–♭5–5–♭7.

Here are some fingering diagrams for the blues scale. Practice each of these patterns until the sound of this scale becomes familiar to you. Note that some of these fingerings require shifting your left hand out of position.

G Blues Scale Fingerings

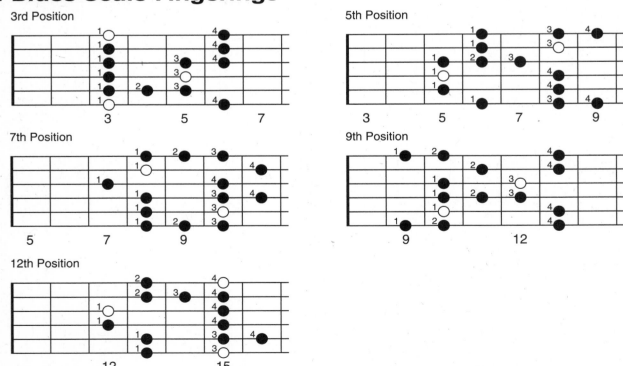

These fingerings are similar to the minor pentatonic fingerings on page 117, but there is one note added.

Eighth-Note Triplets

Some of the following examples will include eighth-note *triplets* to give the solos a more lyrical, flowing quality. A triplet is a rhythmic group of three notes that fit into the duration of two. Eighth notes are generally counted "1–&, 2–&, 3–&, 4–&," but eighth-note triplets are usually counted "1–&–a, 2–&–a, 3–&–a, 4–&–a," or "trip-uh-let, trip-uh-let, trip-uh-let, trip-uh-let."

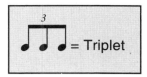

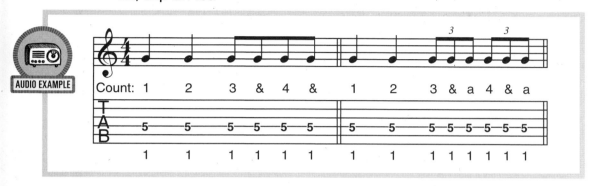

It is important to keep all three notes of the triplet even. Working with a metronome can really help your ability to play triplets accurately at a variety of tempos. Be sure to practice both picking triplets and playing them with hammer-ons and pull-offs. Rhythmic accuracy is very important with all of these techniques.

The next example is a blues/rock solo in the key of G. This solo uses more than one position on the neck, so follow the fingerings carefully. Watch for triplets and count them out slowly if these rhythms are problematic for you.

G Blues/Rock Solo

12-BAR BLUES FORMS

Because rock music has been influenced in a big way by the blues, it is useful for rock guitarists to understand basic blues forms. Perhaps the most common blues form is the *12-bar blues*, which is notated below using *slash notation* (page 98). This type of notation indicates how many beats or bars each chord is played. Slash notation does not show specific rhythms for the chords, and musicians are generally expected to improvise a rhythm that fits the style of the song.

12-Bar Blues in C

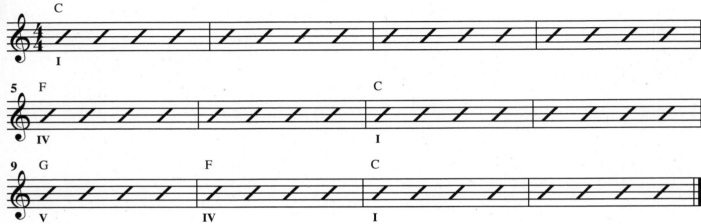

The example above is the most basic representation of the blues form, containing only major triads. Let's look at another variation on this form, which adds the IV chord in measure 2 (called the *quick four*) and a V chord in measure 12. The recorded example ends on the I chord for a sense of finality.

12-Bar Blues in C Variation

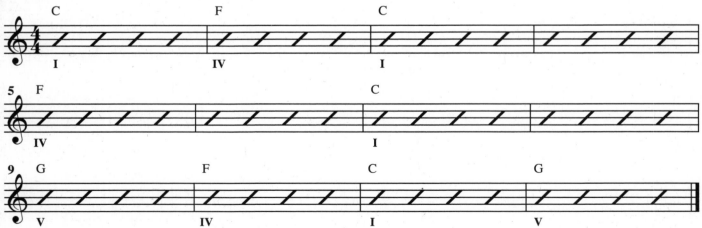

The blues can be built on forms of other lengths too, such as an 8-bar form and a 16-bar form. These are less common than the 12-bar blues, but are still important, especially for musicians interested in blues or jazz.

Now try playing the following example, which is a solo based on the F blues scale over a 12-bar blues in F. It will be played in 7th position, with a single shift out of position for the final note. To find the fingering for this scale, you can simply take the G blues scale fingering in 9th position shown on page 118 and *transpose*, or shift, this pattern down two frets on the fretboard (placing the tonic on the F note rather than the G).

You may find the following example challenging because it uses *syncopated rhythms*, or notes that are played on a weak beat (the "and" or "&" of beat 1 in measure 3, for example) and held over strong beats. Syncopation can be heard in most styles of music and can create rhythmic momentum, or a feeling of pushing forward.

You Ain't Got a Soul to Sell

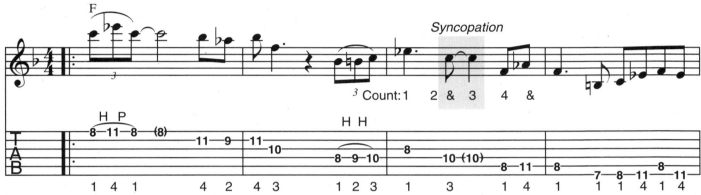

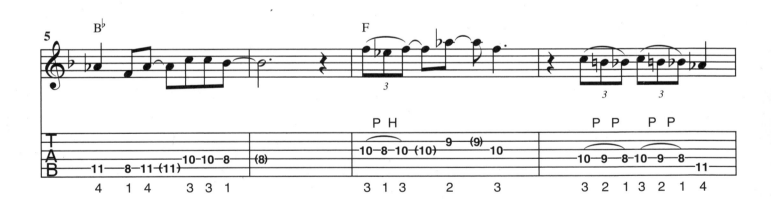

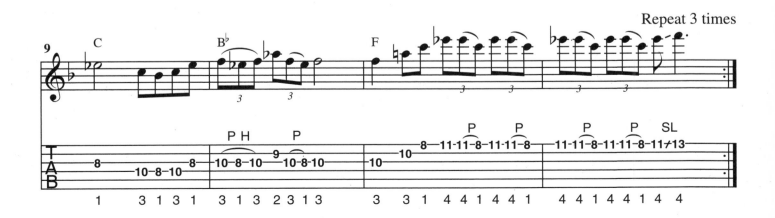

CHOOSING WHICH SCALE TO USE

Now that you have played a few solos with both the minor pentatonic scale and the blues scale, you might be wondering, "How do I know which notes to play or which scale to use?" You can always play either of these scales over a chord that shares the same root. For example, both the E minor pentatonic and E blues scales will work over E minor, E5, and in many cases, E or E7. See the example below comparing these scales and chords.

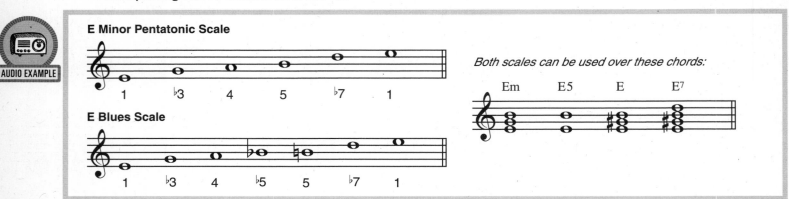

Notice that these scales and chords share some notes; for instance, the notes E and B are present in both scales and in all four chords. In rock music, these scales could also be played over other chords with common notes such as A minor (which contains A and E). It is common for rock guitarists to use one scale even as the chords in the accompaniment change. The most important thing is to use your ear to determine what sounds best.

Here is a solo in D over a V–IV–I–V progression, used in songs like "Takin' Care of Business" by Bachman Turner Overdrive and "She's So Cold" by the Rolling Stones. If it seems that this progression is in the key of A, just remember that a chord progression does not necessarily start on the root note of the key (D in this case). The following example uses the D blues scale and, although it is mostly played in 10th position, contains some position shifts in bars 6 and 7. Pay close attention to the fingerings to make these shifts as easy as possible.

Solo in D

> 8va = *Ottava alta.* Play an octave higher

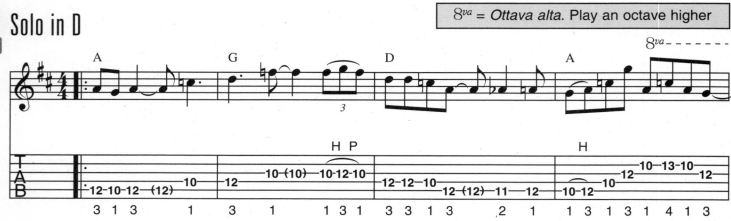

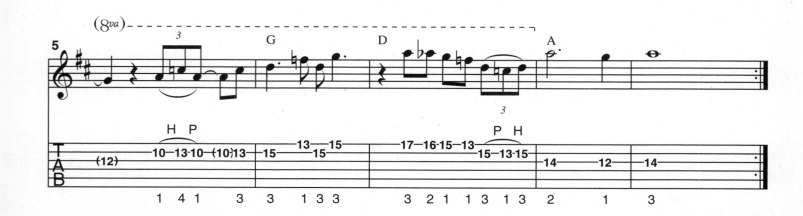

THE MAJOR PENTATONIC SCALE

Like the minor pentatonic scale, the *major pentatonic scale* is a five-note scale that is commonly used for soloing. The following example shows both the C major pentatonic and C minor pentatonic scales. The major pentatonic scale has a brighter, or happier, sound, while the minor pentatonic scale sounds darker, or sadder.

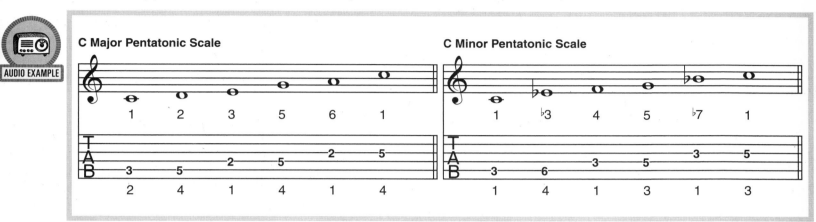

Let's look at some fingerings for this new scale.

C Major Pentatonic Scale Fingerings

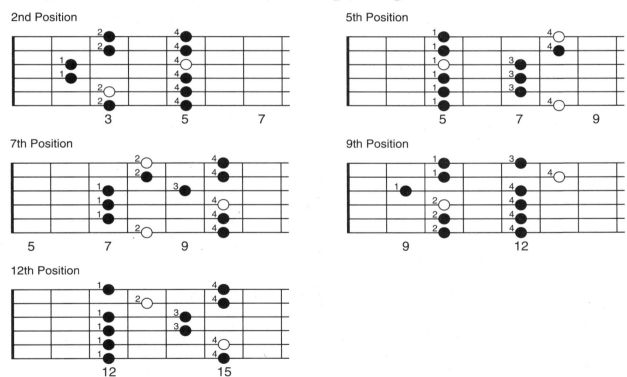

If you look closely, you may notice that the C major pentatonic scale consists of the same notes as the A minor pentatonic scale (page 117). This is because they are *relative* major and minor scales, meaning they use the same exact pitches but have different roots.

SLIDES

When playing lead parts or solos, you can use *slides* to add interest to your playing. There are two types of slides: *legato slides* and *shift slides*. A legato slide is played by picking one note on a string and, while maintaining pressure, sliding your finger along the string to one or more additional notes. Only the first note is picked. A shift slide is played like the legato slide, but both the first and last notes are picked, even those that you have slid into. Below is an example comparing these two techniques.

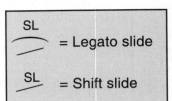

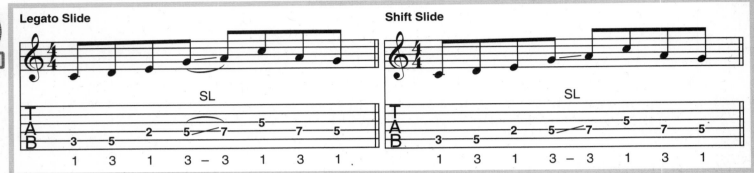

The following solo features slides, eighth-note triplets, syncopation, hammer-ons, and pull-offs. It is constructed from the C major pentatonic scale in the 7th and 9th positions.

Sliding, Slithery Snake

As you've just seen, the major pentatonic scale works well when the key and the scale are rooted on the same note. In the previous solo, you played the C major pentatonic scale over a I–ii–V–IV progression in the key of C. Below is the C major pentatonic scale and some common chords, over which the scale can be played.

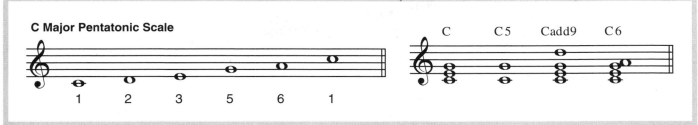

Now, it's time for more playing. The following solo is in the key of B♭, in 5th and 10th position, so you can transpose the 7th and 12 position fingerings from page 123 down two frets for this example.

When It Rains, It's Red

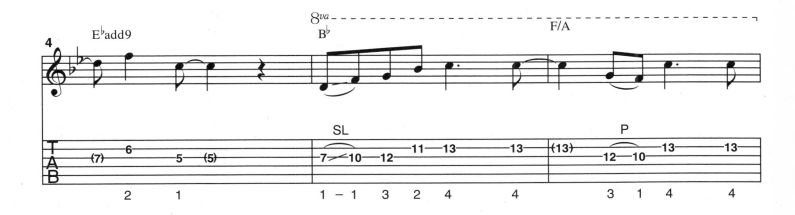

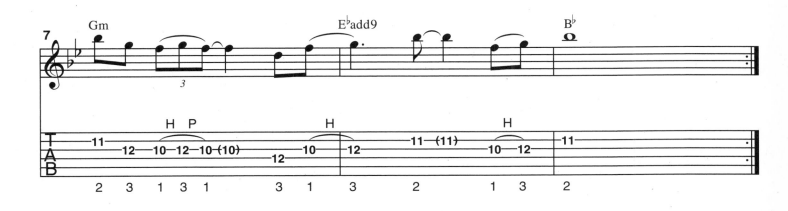

Sixteenth Notes

Another note value that can be quite useful for solos and lead guitar parts is the *sixteenth note*. A sixteenth note lasts ½ the duration of an eighth note, or ¼ of a beat in $\frac{4}{4}$ time.

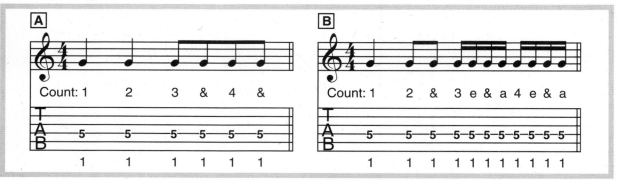

Try playing the above exercise with a metronome set to click on every quarter note. Counting sixteenth notes with the syllables "e–&–a" can help ensure that you are hearing and playing four equal divisions of the quarter note. When playing sixteenth notes, it helps to use alternate picking (page 62). Remember, this means using down strokes (⊓ downward motions of the pick) for the downbeat and "&," and using up strokes (∨ upward motions of the pick) for the "e" and "a." This constant down–up motion will help you play more efficiently.

The following solo will give you a chance to practice playing sixteenth notes in a musical context using the D major pentatonic scale in 7th position over a I–IV–I–V progression. The fingerings are based on the 5th-position fingering of the C major pentatonic scale, moved up two frets.

Malodorous Mama

Practice playing sixteenth notes in other situations, including over the backing tracks for the scales and solos covered so far in this book. When learning any new rhythms, the goal is to play in time as accurately as possible. Do not rush when playing sixteenth notes, and remember to slow down your metronome as much as necessary to get completely comfortable with this rhythm before increasing the tempo.

PHRASING TIPS

Now that you have learned a few of the most common scales used in rock soloing, let's take a step back and discuss the larger issue of *phrasing*. This is a complex concept, one that can be tricky to define. Phrasing can be thought of as the art of performing so that the notes sound as though they belong together and the musical ideas relate to one another. Musicians who have mastered this art understand a wide variety of musical concepts and possibilities. Let's break down the broad idea of phrasing into some more practically applicable tools: Rhythmic Imitation; Using Rests Effectively; Varying Dynamics and Tone; and Exploring the Full Range of Pitch.

Rhythmic Imitation

Using rhythm creatively can be one way to play a well-developed solo. Here is an example of rhythmic imitation using the G minor pentatonic scale in various positions (with the addition of the note A in measure 9) over a progression in G minor. Listen to the way the guitar solo borrows and imitates rhythms played by the bass.

Wheelin' and Stealin'

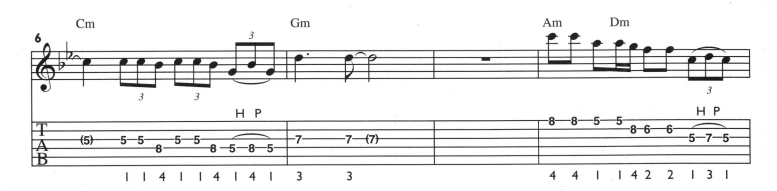

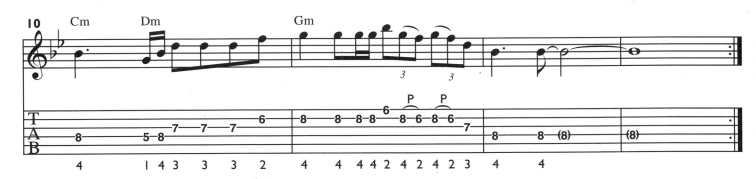

Try imitating rhythms played by other instruments the next time you solo. Also, try mimicking the rhythm of the main melody of a song; this can be a great way to tie your solo into the entire composition. There are many options here and all are well worth exploring. Like anything else in music, you never know where your experiments might lead.

Using Rests Effectively

Without rests, your solos might sound like musical run-on sentences, which will ultimately serve only to confuse your listeners. Look at the two examples below; the first is overloaded with ideas, while the second strikes an even balance between notes and rests. Both solos are played with the D♭ major pentatonic scale in 3rd position over a I–V–IV–I progression in D♭. As these examples show, playing without rests can be effective for building intensity for a short period of time, but a prolonged absence of rests might sound like a technical exercise, not music.

Without Rests

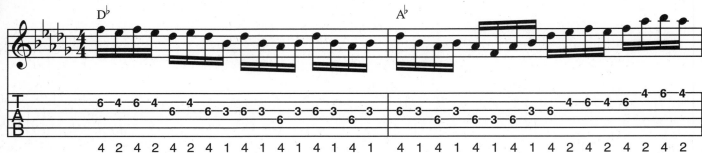

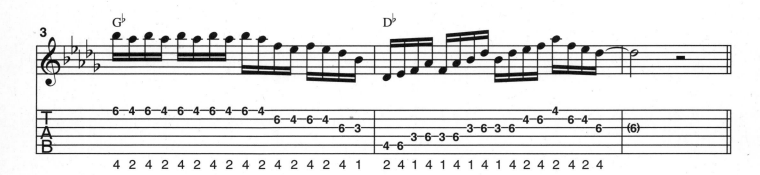

With Rests

Varying Dynamics and Tone

Dynamics (page 54, variation in volume) and *tone* (the quality of an instrument's sound) are two ways to keep your sound fresh throughout the course of a song. While it is common to hear guitarists use a softer, less distorted tone when not soloing or playing lead parts, a thorough exploration of dynamics is often lacking in rock music, particularly since it has become fashionable to mix recordings at a constant, usually loud, dynamic level.

The following chart shows the more common dynamic markings used in music, along with their definitions. These abbreviations come from Italian terms, which are shown on the right in italics.

Common Dynamics

pp = *pianissimo* (very quiet)

p = *piano* (quiet)

mp = *mezzo piano* (moderately quiet)

mf = *mezzo forte* (moderately loud)

f = *forte* (loud)

ff = *fortissimo* (very loud)

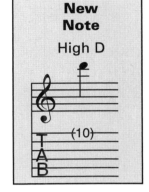

New Note

High D

The following solo uses the B minor pentatonic scale in 7th position over a two-chord vamp. Notice that there are dynamic indications in the music, which you will hear on the recording.

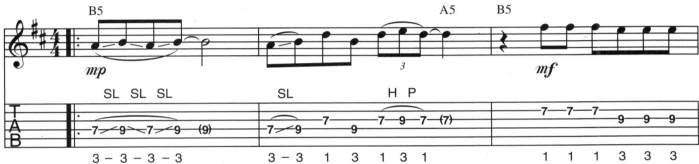

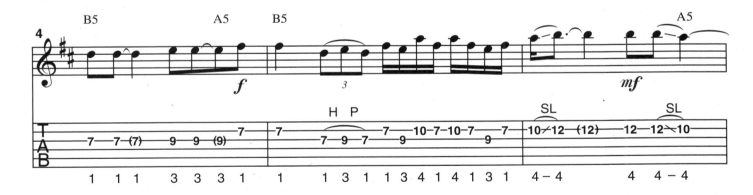

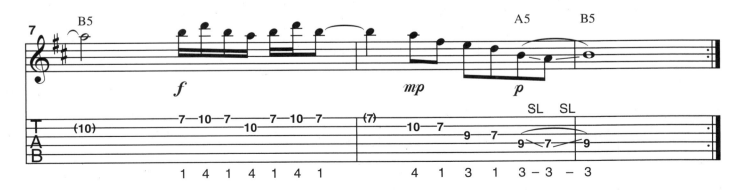

Exploring Full Range of Pitch

Another great way to keep your solos engaging is to explore a wide range of pitch. While it is often impractical to incorporate the highest and lowest possible pitches on the guitar into a solo, using several positions and extremes of pitch can sound fantastic if done tastefully. The following solo uses the C blues scale in several positions on the neck over a simplified blues progression.

New Note

High E♭

Up and Down Your Spine

You may find that solos often follow this form; beginning in the low register, continuing up to the high register, and finally ending in the low register again.

ROCK TECHNIQUE

Bending

If you have listened to or played rock music for very long at all, you have heard *bending*. Bends are very popular and can give your solos a vocal-like quality. Light gauge strings (.010"–.046") work well for bending, but if your hands are strong enough, you can use any gauge and still bend. Don't forget to reinforce bends with additional fingers; if you are bending a note fretted with your 3rd finger, use the 2nd finger to assist the bend.

Before using bends in a solo, it is a good idea to develop bending precision, especially if you haven't done too much bending in the past. Here is an exercise that's great for pitch accuracy when bending. First, play a fretted note to get the sound in your ear; this will be your target pitch. Then, slide down one half step and bend this lower note up one half step to the target pitch. Repeat as many times as necessary to bend that half step accurately. From there, move on to more challenging bends. Next, try bending from a whole step or even three half steps (one-and-a-half steps) below to the target pitch.

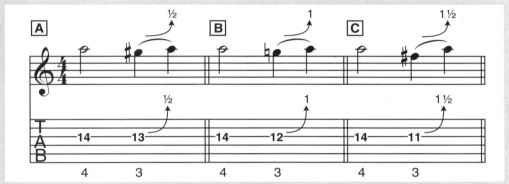
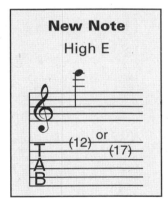

If you're ready to try something more challenging, move on to the next exercise. It will test your ability to bend accurately with a cool descending lick in E.

Bending Exercise

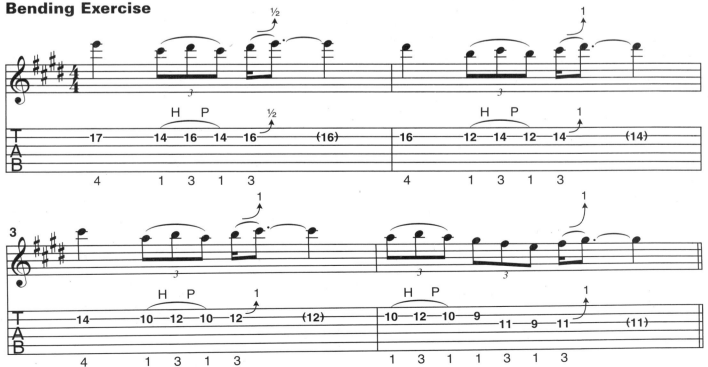

Now that you're comfortable bending notes up, it's time to practice bending and releasing notes to their original pitches. In the following exercise, after each note is bent, it is released to the original pitch. Do not pick the note a second time when you release it to the original pitch.

Bend and Release

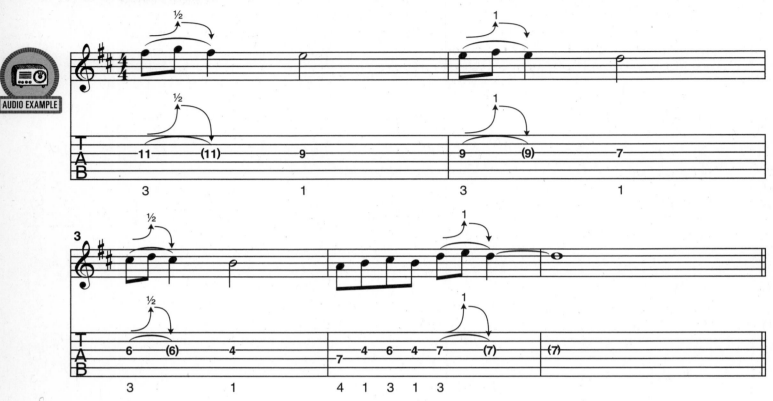

Grace Notes

Grace notes are ornamental notes used in rock guitar solos to add rhythmic drive and accent important notes. Grace notes are notated with smaller noteheads, and are not counted because their rhythmic value is borrowed from the note they precede. Listen to the following C♯ minor pentatonic lick played once without grace notes, and once with grace notes.

♪ = Grace note

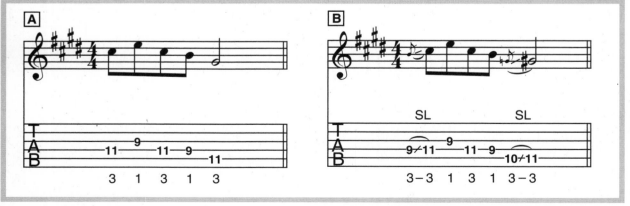

By simply adding two grace notes, you've really spiced things up!

Vibrato

A close relative of bending is *vibrato*, or a slight wavering of pitch used to add emotion to a phrase. Vibrato can be used to make fretted notes and even bent notes sustain longer. On the guitar, there are three types of vibrato: *classical vibrato*, *blues vibrato*, and *whammy bar vibrato*. Classical vibrato involves rocking your left hand back and forth along the length of the string. Blues, or bending, vibrato is applied by rapidly bending and releasing a note. Vibrato with a whammy bar is similar to blues vibrato, in that it involves bending and releasing, but the vibrato has a different quality. It is also possible to add uniform vibrato to an entire chord with the whammy bar. This can be done with our other two forms of vibrato, but it is physically easier to use the whammy bar for this purpose.

Listen to these three vibrato types in action using the same C♯ minor pentatonic lick from the last example.

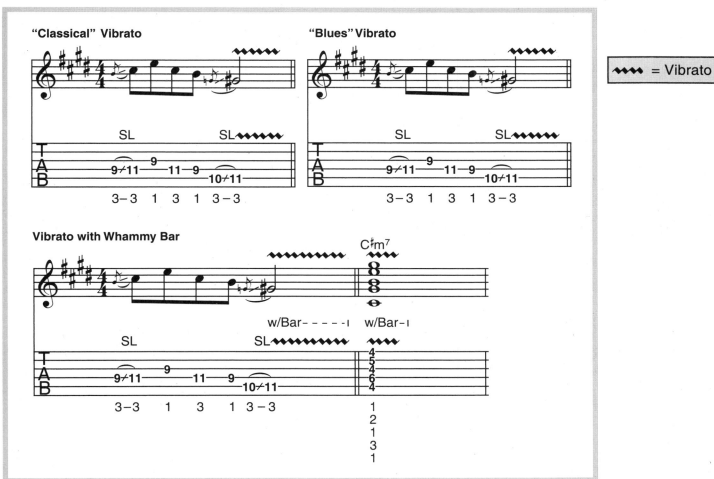

The solo on the next page is in the style of Tom Scholz (of the band Boston) and features bends, grace notes, vibrato, and more. Be aware that some of the bends are released to their original pitch. Although this example starts with a G♯ minor chord, it ends with a B chord, so it is considered to be in the key of B.

AUDIO EXAMPLE

Prepare to Launch

Quarter-Step Bends

To get a bluesy or gritty sound, guitarists will often incorporate *quarter-step bends*, or bends to pitches that are between the 12 notes used in Western music. Compare the following two licks in the key of F minor. The only difference between them is the bend interval—a half step in the first instance and a quarter step in the second instance.

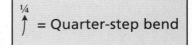
= Quarter-step bend

AUDIO EXAMPLE

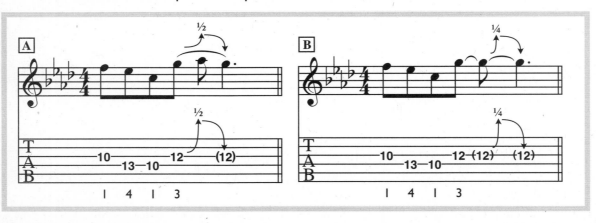

ROCK LICKS IN THE STYLES OF THE MASTERS

In the Style of Eric Clapton

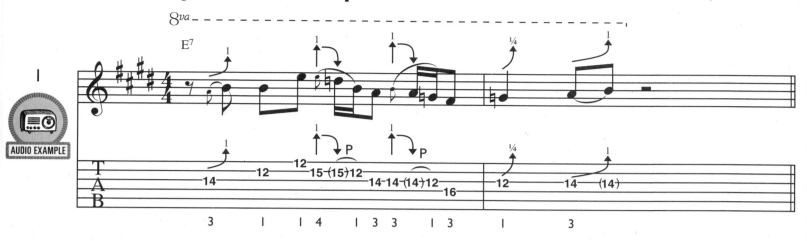

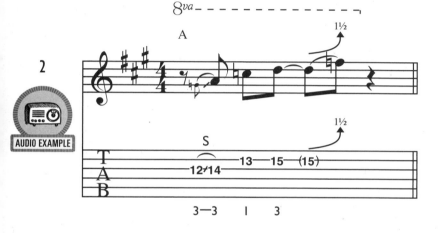

> **DID YOU KNOW?** Nicknamed "Slowhand" by his band, The Yardbirds, Eric Clapton is often viewed as one of the greatest guitarists of all time.

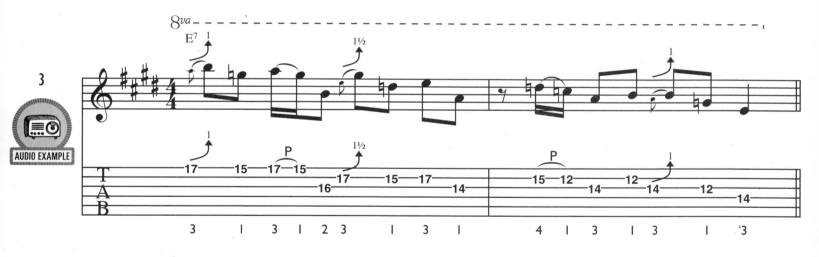

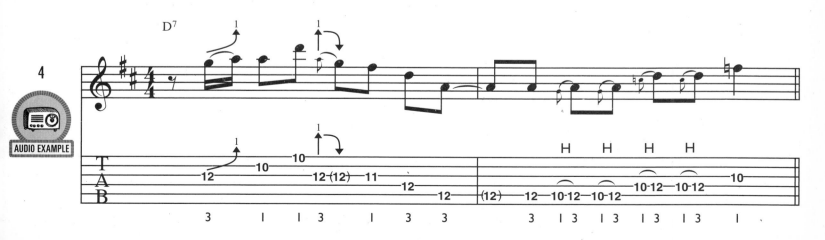

In the Style of Jimi Hendrix

Perhaps the most celebrated guitarist of all time, Jimi Hendrix changed the sound of rock guitar playing forever. Jimi's style stemmed from his blues background. He used pentatonic scales as a framework, and also incorporated double stops, arpeggios and modes into his musical arsenal. But, of course, it wasn't the notes he played that made him great, it was how he played them.

In the Style of Jimmy Page

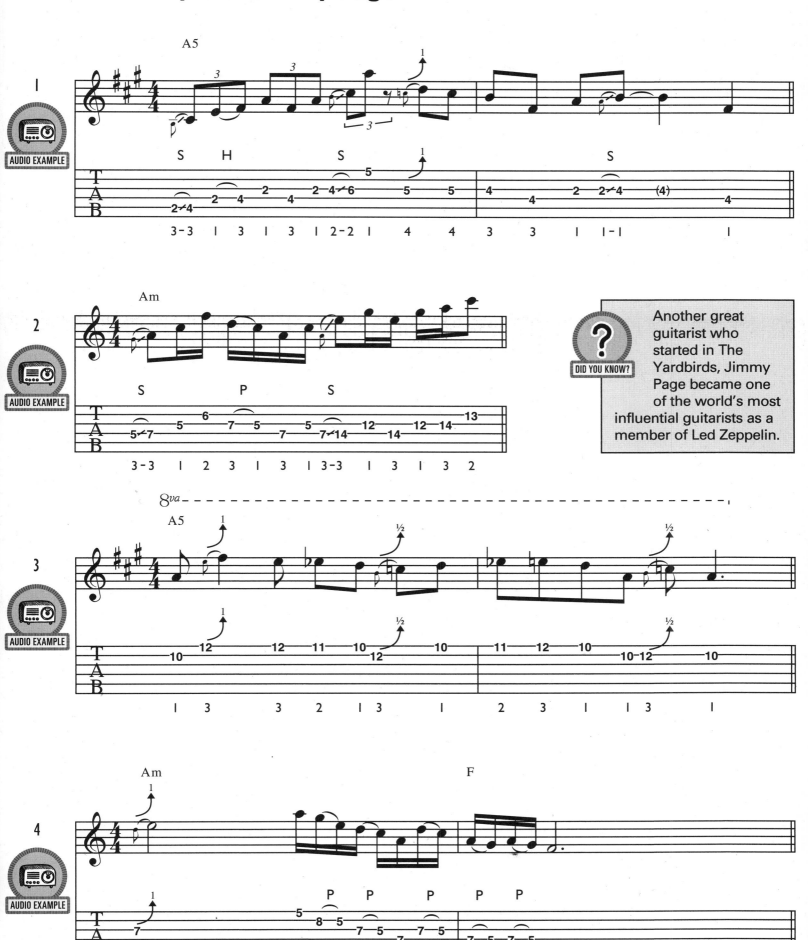

Another great guitarist who started in The Yardbirds, Jimmy Page became one of the world's most influential guitarists as a member of Led Zeppelin.

In the Style of Carlos Santana

Carlos Santana's real name is Carlos Humberto Santana de Barragan, and he was born in Mexico in 1947. He became famous in the 1960s and 1970s with his band, Santana.

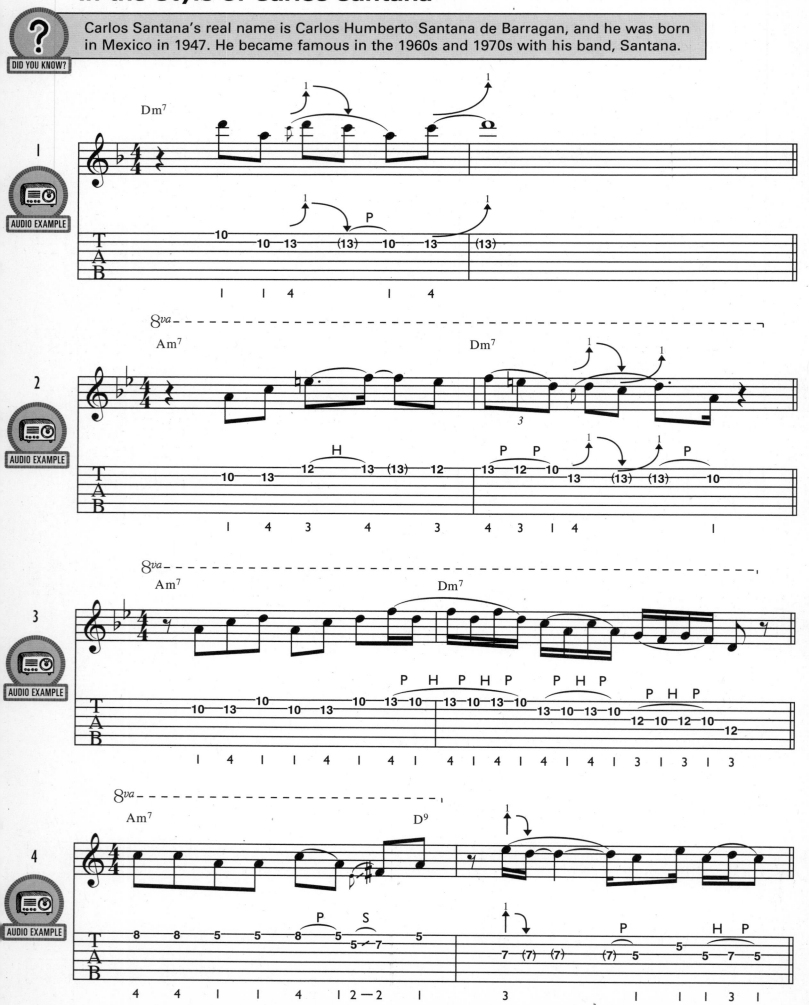

In the Style of Kirk Hammett

Kirk Hammett, born in 1962, is the lead guitarist for Metallica. His sound is influenced by jazz, blues and classical styles.

Notice the nested sixteenth-note triplet in the fourth beat of the first full measure in this lick. The third eighth in an eighth-note triplet is divided into three equal sixteenth notes.

JAM TRACKS

The following pages (141–146) contain jam tracks for you to play along with to practice your improvising. They are backing tracks—your very own back-up band! Spend as many hours as you can jamming with them; use them to learn your scales, try out new licks, and just for fun! No matter how much fun you have, you'll be making yourself a better lead guitarist.

Each jam track comes with a lead sheet showing which chords are being played and the form of the tune so you can follow along. It's a good idea to just listen all the way through once while following the music, just to become familiar with the sound and the form. You can also begin formulating ideas for the kinds of things you want to try to play as you jam over the track.

You'll find scale fretboard diagrams (as described on page 114) with each track. These are the scale forms you should use to play a lead guitar solo with the band. This is the best, most fun way to learn new scales.

It's also a good idea to practice playing rhythm guitar with each track. All of the chords you'll need to know can be found in the chord dictionary starting on page 176.

Have fun!

Slash Notation

As you learned on page 98, slash notation is used as a substitution for standard music notation or rhythmic notation. When you see slash notation, you can choose to play any rhythm you like. Four slashes in a measure simply indicate that there are four beats in the measure. For example, this line of music has four beats per measure:

J. B. Goode's Blues

Each time the progression is played is called a *chorus*. There are 21 choruses in this jam track. The form is shown at the bottom of the page. You'll be playing with a full rhythm section (drums, bass, keys) and another guitarist. Enjoy!

A Minor Pentatonic

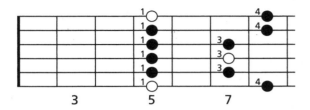

A Major Pentatonic

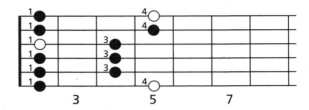

Fast Blues in A

Chorus 1:   INTRO

Chorus 2–10:   You solo

Chorus 11:   INTRO repeats, 2nd guitar has riff and solo

Chorus 12:   You solo

Chorus 13:   2nd guitar solos

Chorus 14:   You solo

Chorus 15:   2nd guitar solos

Chorus 16:   You solo

Chorus 17:   Rhythm section plays, you may solo or play rhythm guitar

Chorus 18–20: You solo

Chorus 21:   INTRO repeats, standard ending

K. C.'s Blues

Notice that this track includes piano and organ, as well as a second guitarist. Have fun jamming with this infectious groove!

C Minor Pentatonic

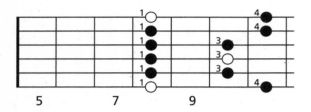

C Major Pentatonic

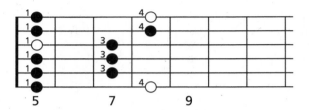

Shuffle Blues in C

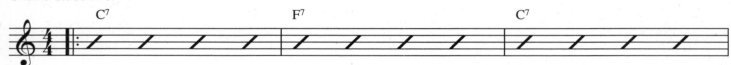

Chorus 1:	INTRO
Chorus 2–3:	You solo
Chorus 4:	Piano solos
Chorus 5–6:	You solo
Chorus 7:	2nd guitar solos
Chorus 8–9:	You solo
Chorus 10:	Organ solos
Chorus 11–12:	You solo
Chorus 13:	Last chorus, long ending

Eddie's Rock

Fans of Van Halen and '80s rock, in general, will have a blast with this one. The form is built right into the music, so no separate form chart is needed. Since this one is in the key of C major, the C major and C major pentatonic scales will do the trick.

C Minor Pentatonic

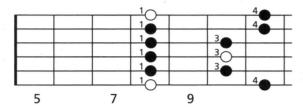

C Major Pentatonic

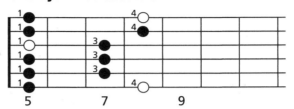

Moderate Rock

Intro: No drums or guitar

Intro: No drums or guitar

Play 8 times

144

Dorian Rock

Dorian is a *mode* of the major scale. A mode is a reordering of a scale. To jam over this funky rock track, you'll use the D Dorian mode, which is simply the C major scale starting and ending on the note D. It's a beautiful minor sound and a favorite of the rock guitar legend Carlos Santana.

D Dorian Mode

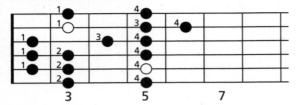

Moderate Funk

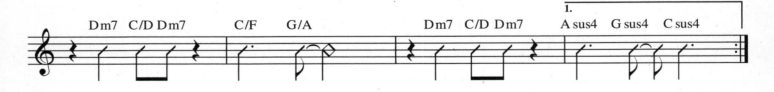

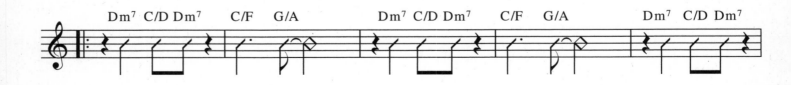

Phrygian Rock

Phrygian is another *mode* of the major scale. This track is in E and has a minor sound, so the E Phrygian mode will work perfectly. E Phrygian is simply the C major scale played starting and ending on the note E. The Phrygian mode has a very exotic, Spanish or even Middle Eastern sound and is commonly used in metal rock.

E Phrygian Mode

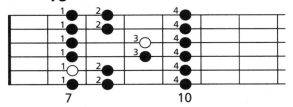

Moderate Fast Rock

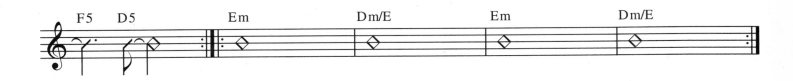

Jeff's Jam

This tune is in the style of the '70s rock classic, "Freeway Jam" by Jeff Beck. It is perfect for the Mixolydian mode, which is yet another mode of the major scale. The G Mixolydian mode can be found by simply playing the C major scale starting and ending on G.

G Mixolydian Mode

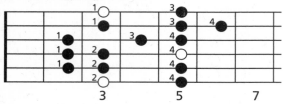

Moderate Shuffle

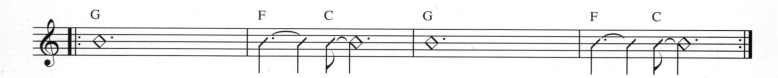

PART 3: BEING A PROFESSIONAL GUITARIST

Playing the guitar in a band is fun and rewarding. Having acquired the skills and knowledge offered in this book so far, you are probably ready to play in a band. This section of the book provides tips on starting or joining a band, preparing for an audition, rehearsing and gigging. You'll also learn how to promote yourself, and even how to practice more effectively. Finally, you'll gain some insights into the music business, discover how to protect your interests and eventually get a recording contract. Let's get started.

FINDING, REHEARSING AND PROMOTING A BAND

How to Tell If You're Ready To Play in a Band

If you can play over a dozen songs from beginning to end without many mistakes and without losing the beat, then you are ready to play in a band. For a band to play live, they need to know at least a dozen songs.

How to Start a Band

There are a number of ways to find other musicians to play with. One way is to ask an instructor if he or she has any students who might want to get together with you. Most instructors want to help their students find other people to play with, and they may already know who to suggest. This method can help you find other guitarists as well as bass players, drummers, keyboard players and any other kind of musician.

Another way to find musicians to play with is to put up an ad at your local music store. Make it brief and to the point, saying what type of players you are looking for. You can put the same ad in your local paper or classified Website. Many classified sections will charge nothing for this service.

How to Find and Get into an Existing Band

It's a good idea to talk to people that you know in the music business and ask if they know of a band that is looking for a guitarist. If they're not aware of any at the time, ask if they can keep you in mind and recommend you, or at least, let you know the next time they hear of an opening. You can make a personal webpage which tells about your experience, musical preferences, and equipment. Have business cards made which include your phone number, e-mail address and webpage address. Musicians tend to help each other, and hopefully someday you'll be in a position to return the favor.

Other ways of finding bands looking for guitarists are to look on bulletin boards in music stores and look in classified ads in newspapers and music magazines. You can also find bands that need guitarists on the Internet. To access a number of musician referral services on the Internet, search: musician+referral service.

TIPS

How to Be the One Everyone Wants in Their Band

1. **Show up at all rehearsals on time.** When it's time to start, have your guitar already tuned, your amp set and be ready to go. This shows that you are enthusiastic about playing.

2. **Have your parts learned well.** Have the song arrangements memorized. Be ready to play the songs all the way through without making a lot of mistakes. Do as much preparation as possible outside of rehearsal.

3. **Have a good attitude.** Be enthusiastic about the group and about rehearsals. A positive attitude is contagious. If you're excited about playing, the other members will pick up on it and will become enthusiastic themselves.

4. **Be a team player.** Leave your ego outside the door. Keep in mind that everyone in the group is working towards a common goal. Have respect for the other members and their opinions.

5. **Help with the business of the band.** Do all you can to help with band promotion, getting gigs and keeping track of the finances. Remember that being in a band is being part of a business.

6. **When you're not playing a song, don't play.** Just turn your volume off. This rule applies to rehearsals, sound checks and performances. Don't play at all between songs. Playing between songs can be distracting and annoying to other members of the group and to the audience.

7. **Never tune your guitar aloud.** Use a silent electronic tuner, one that cuts off the signal to your amp while you tune.

8. **Learn to sing.** Finding players who can sing is a big challenge for many bands. Knowing how to sing, even a little, can be the difference between you and the other guy getting the job.

Your Personal Promotional Pack

In order to join almost any established band, you will need to try to get an audition with that band. In order to get an audition, you may need to have your own *promo pack*.

What Your Promo Pack Should Include

Your promo pack should contain:

- A photograph of yourself,

- A recording that has two or three minutes of your best playing,

- A biography that tells about your experience.

Make your promo pack as professional-looking as possible by having a good photographer take your picture, and have it enlarged into an 8x10 glossy. The recording should be one with songs that you have recorded in the studio and include parts of any songs that best demonstrate your abilities. If you can play in some different styles, be sure to include them on your recording. Versatility is always good.

If you haven't been in the studio, record yourself playing something at home that you can play well and shows your ability. Remember, most bands are looking for a player who can play solid rhythm guitar as well as lead, so be sure to put something on your tape that shows you can play solid rhythm and not just solos. If there is a specific group for which you would like to audition, think of the kind of guitarist that they may be looking for and make a tape especially for that group.

How to Prepare for an Audition

Learning to audition well can be a huge asset to your musical career. A successful band will have several guitarists competing for the position. Here are some tips that could make the difference between you getting the job and someone else getting it:

1. **Be well prepared.** When preparing for an audition, spend every spare minute learning the songs that you'll play at the audition. Play the songs over and over until you can play them in your sleep.

2. **Learn as much of the band's material as possible.** *Extra effort shows a good attitude and can be the reason that you are hired.* Show the band that if they were to hire you, you would be ready to start playing shows with only one or two rehearsals. In most cases, there will only be time for one or two rehearsals, so a successful band will need to work you in as quickly as possible.

3. **Your attitude can be as important as your playing.** The band will want to hire someone with a positive attitude, who is enthusiastic about the band and their music. When a band is looking for someone to hire, they know that they are going to be dealing with that person on a daily basis. Leave your ego at home when you are auditioning. If you are willing to relocate, be sure to tell them this. This can be a major factor in the decision of whether or not to hire you. The bottom line at an audition is that most of the time the person who gets the job is the person who wants it the most—the person with the "whatever it takes" attitude. Not all successful bands are looking for a jaded pro who has "been there, done that." A good attitude can compensate for lack of experience. Most bands are looking for members who are hungry for success. So, don't worry if you haven't played a thousand live shows or been on lots of albums. Despite your lack of experience, you could still be exactly the person they are looking for.

    Good luck!

What You May Be Asked to Play at an Audition

At most auditions, you will be asked to play some of the band's material. You may or may not be told ahead of time which songs you will play. You may be given a few minutes with a recording of a song to see how well you can learn it in a short period of time. It's likely that you'll be asked to play some of your own material as well, so have a few things prepared that you think will fit with the style of the band. The band may be interested in your songwriting style as well as your playing ability and attitude.

Equipment to Bring to an Audition

Bring a spare guitar to the audition. This way, if you should happen to break a string, everyone won't have to wait while you change it; you can just pick up your spare. Also bring a spare guitar cable, an extension chord and a *ground lift* (an adapter that allows you to plug a three-prong plug into a two-prong outlet). By bringing the extension chord and ground lift, you know you'll be able to plug in your amp, which is a problem you don't want to have to deal with at the start of an audition. Change your strings the day before and make sure that all of your cables work. Before your audition, make sure that all of your equipment is in good working order. This is another way to show your professionalism.

Rehearsing and Improving the Band

Rehearsal Location

You can rehearse just about any place where you can play loudly without disturbing the neighbors. The ideal situation is one where you can leave your equipment set up and just walk in and start playing. If you can't rehearse at someone's house, check the phone book to find a rehearsal facility near you. Rehearsal facilities charge by the hour, by the day or by the month. A good way to save some money is to share the rehearsal space with another band and split the rent.

PHOTO • BOB GRUEN/COURTESY OF STAR FILE, INC.

In their early days (1970), **Aerosmith** rehearsed in the basement of their apartment building located at 1325 Commonwealth Avenue in Boston. In 1971, they began rehearsing at Boston's unheated Fenway Theatre, where they showcased for Frank Connoly, the agent that eventually helped them land a recording contract with Columbia Records.

Tips for Making Rehearsals More Productive

1. **Have an agenda.** Decide on the songs to be rehearsed a few days before the rehearsal. Make sure that everyone has recordings of all relevant material.

2. **Don't be afraid to stop a song if there is a problem.** Go over the problem part a few times if necessary. Make sure everyone is clear on exactly how that part should go.

3. **Don't beat a song into the ground by playing it over and over.** After playing a song more than a few times, it becomes easy to lose your focus. It is more productive to move on, even if you haven't perfected the song yet. Then, come back to it after a while. This keeps rehearsals productive and also keeps the band from burning out on a song.

4. **Record your rehearsals.** Then listen to the recording and try to find which parts need more work. Do this as a group, if possible. This can be as productive as actual rehearsal because the band can discuss how to fix any weak spots. It can be easier to hear the weak spots while listening to a recording than to hear them when the band is playing. It's also much easier to stop the recording than it is to stop the band in the middle of a song to make a comment.

5. **Be sure that all song intros and endings are solid.** The audience may or may not hear a mistake made during the song, but a mistake in the very beginning or at the very end of the song will be the most noticeable.

6. **Band Members Only at Rehearsal.** The only people who should be at a rehearsal are the members of the band. Your rehearsals will be much more productive this way, because when there is even one other person in the room, the rehearsal becomes a performance. Constructive criticism between members becomes more difficult because no one wants to be corrected or criticized in front of an audience.

People outside the band will always want to watch you rehearse. Politely tell them that your band's rehearsals are "closed." Once you have the entire show together, an open rehearsal with some invited friends can be a good opportunity to try out a live show on an audience. An open rehearsal is more of a performance than a rehearsal and should only be done when the band feels like they are ready to perform.

7. **Controlling Dynamics.** *Dynamics* refers to varying the degrees of volume. One mark of a good guitarist is the ability to know when to get louder or softer. Dynamics can be controlled in several ways. One is by the use of a volume knob or pedal, and another is by how hard or soft one hits the strings. Also, the use of *palm muting* (laying the right side of your right palm gently across the strings near the bridge) is an effective way to control dynamics.

8. **A Good Way to Get Your Band Members Motivated** Book a gig. Having a show coming up will give everyone in the band something to anticipate and work toward. However, be sure that the band has enough time to prepare for it.

How Long to Rehearse Before You Play Your First Gig

Before you play your first gig, you should have rehearsed the songs until you are just starting to get bored playing them. If you know a song well enough to be bored playing it, then you know it well enough to play it live. The band will probably be somewhat nervous during its first performance. The more automatic the songs are, the less chances there are of making mistakes due to nerves.

Getting Ready for the Gig

The more prepared you are for a show, the more fun you'll have. You will be able to focus on enjoying yourself as well as focusing on what you are playing. You will always play your best when you don't have to think about what you're playing.

How to Get Gigs for Your Band

The Band's Promo Pack

In order for your band to get gigs you will need to have a promo pack. The band's promo pack should contain:

1. **A CD or tape of the band.** If your band has a CD, include one in your promo pack. If it doesn't, record three of your best songs and include the recording in your promo pack. Club owners won't want to spend a lot of time listening to your demo so three songs will be plenty.

2. **A photo of the band.** You can either get creative here or have a simple photo of the band. If you choose to get creative, be sure that the photo reflects the style of music that you play.

3. **A brief history of the band, including:**
   A. A description of the style of music that the band plays
   B. The names of the band members and what instrument they play
   C. A list of songs that the band plays
   D. A list of places that the band has played before
   E. Anything interesting about the band

4. **Any newspaper articles, reviews or press about the band.**
   Good press or reviews about the band are a great addition to a promo pack. Photocopy any articles or pictures and include the name and date of the newspaper or magazine in which they appeared.

5. **The name and number of the businessperson for the band.** For example, "for booking and information, contact John Smith at (555) 555-5555." *Be sure that this number is given in several places in the promo pack,* especially on the recording package and on the photo. In case parts of the kit get separated, they will still be able to contact you. You will need to have an answering machine for your contact number so that the person who may want to book your band can leave a message. Remember that your promo pack reflects your band and its professionalism.

How to Use a Promo Pack

Give copies of your promo pack to the managers of clubs or other places that your band could play. It's also a good idea to give copies to booking agents because a good booking agent will be able to find you more gigs than you would be able to find on your own. The booking agent will charge a fee for each gig that he or she books. This may be a flat fee or a percentage of what the band is paid. You should also give copies of your promo pack to magazines and newspapers; they may want to do a review or a story on your band.

The Gig

How to Get Ready Backstage

Here's a routine that will help you warm-up and get in the right frame of mind to perform. Start with stretching until you feel limber. Then start warming up on your guitar. Play chords, licks and scales, starting slowly and gradually speeding up until your hands feel loose and ready to go. Don't go overboard, though. You could fatigue your hands before the show, which defeats the purpose of warming up. You may be nervous before a performance. Deep breathing and stretching exercises can be helpful for overcoming pre-performance jitters.

Words to Keep in Mind to Help Give Your Best Performance

Instead of thinking, "let me *impress* the audience," think, "let me *entertain* the audience." Your main jobs when you're performing live are to have fun and entertain the audience. If you are having fun and are playing like there's no place you'd rather be than on stage, your audience will pick up on that attitude and enjoy watching you play.

What to Do If You Make a Mistake

There are two kinds of mistakes: arrangement mistakes and playing mistakes. An arrangement mistake is when a player forgets how the song is supposed to go and, for example, plays the wrong section of the song at the wrong time. Arrangement mistakes are usually more noticeable and are a sign that the song still needs some work. If you know your songs well, you shouldn't be making these kinds of errors.

A playing mistake is when a player plays the wrong note or chord. These mistakes are a basic part of life—even the best players make them from time to time—and are usually easy to cover up. However, if you are making more than one playing mistake every few songs, you may want to practice your parts on your own, just to refresh them.

If you make a mistake when you're performing, just relax and jump back into the song. Try not to make a face or do anything that would let the audience know that you made a mistake. Chances are, unless the mistake is really obvious, no one will even notice. Don't dwell on the mistake, just continue in the song as if it never happened. Thinking about a mistake after you make it will only distract you and cause you to make even more mistakes.

How to Make Your Mistakes Less Noticeable

It's normal to make mistakes, but one thing you can do to make your mistakes less obvious is to play right through them. The way to practice this is to pretend you are performing. Play the song from start to finish and play right through any mistakes you might make. When you are playing by yourself, you may be tempted to stop when you make a mistake. Try to resist this temptation. The golden rule of performing is this: *No matter what happens, don't stop during the song.* When you are practicing a song from start to finish, follow this rule just as you would during a performance.

Practice Playing the Songs without Looking

The less you look at your guitar, the more eye contact you can have with the audience. Playing the songs without looking shows that you have confidence in what you are doing. However, there are certain times when you should look at your guitar. For example, when you are shifting from one part of the fretboard to another, it is better to watch where you are going than to make the jump without looking, which could cause you to land on the wrong fret. After you practice without looking for a while, you'll start to get a feel for where the notes are on the fretboard.

PHOTO • BOB GRUEN/COURTESY OF STAR FILE, INC.

DID YOU KNOW?

Before joining the Yardbirds in the mid 1960s and forming Led Zeppelin in 1968, *Jimmy Page* made a name for himself in London as a session musician.
He plays most of the time without looking, making his playing seem natural and effortless.

GET BETTER, SOONER

Getting Warmed Up

One of the most important parts of a practice session is the warm-up. Playing vigorously without warming up can cause injury. Just as an athlete warms up before a strenuous workout, we must warm-up our fingers before strenuous playing.

To warm up properly, all of the muscle groups you use to play should be warmed-up slowly. Different muscle groups are used to play different things. For example, we use different muscles on the fretting hand for bending strings than for playing chords. Each of these different groups of muscles must be warmed up.

The key words for warming up are *slow* and *easy*. Let your hands gradually stretch out and get your circulation going. Start slowly and gradually increase the intensity of your playing. Starting slowly has two benefits. The first is that it allows your muscles to warm-up gradually. The second is that it will keep you relaxed. Tight muscles are enemies of speed and accuracy.

Your warm-up routine could start with scales or picking exercises, then move to string bending and licks and finish with strumming. Warming up usually takes between ten and fifteen minutes but can vary depending on how often you play. The longer the periods of time between practice sessions, the longer (and slower) your warm-ups should be.

Practicing

Setting-Up Your Practice Area

The best place to practice is someplace where you won't be disturbed. Your practice area should be a place where you can get away from the rest of the world and have "your time." If you are lucky, you'll have a place where you can leave all of your materials ready to use. Even a small corner of a room will do.

What You'll Need in Your Practice Area

When you're getting ready to play, have everything that you might need within reach. This way you won't have to interrupt your train of thought just to get up and get something you need. Here are some things to keep handy in your practice area:

TIPS

1. Recording media (tapes, CDRs, whatever you use)
2. Recording device
3. Playback device (CD player, tape player, etc.)
4. Metronome or drum machine
5. Picks
6. Blank fretboard charts
7. Pencil with eraser
8. Any books or magazines that you want to work with
9. Tuner
10. Spare set of strings and a peg winder (in case you break a string)
11. Something to drink

What and How Much to Practice

When you are deciding what to practice, consider both long-term and short-term goals as a player. Your short-term goal may be to learn a song that you like or to master a new technique. Your long-term goals may range from playing for a few friends to becoming a successful recording artist. Whatever your goals are, and they may change often, try to select areas of study that will help you reach your goals. If one of your goals is to become a well-rounded player, it is important to vary your areas of study and not work on the same things during each practice session. Here is a short list of things to consider:

GIVE IT A TRY

Arpeggios
Bending and vibrato
Chords
Ear training
Improvising
Lead guitar
Learning new songs
New chords

Note naming
Phrasing
Playing songs from a songbook
Practicing songs that you know
Scales
Songwriting
Technique exercises
Timing and rhythm

Before you start practicing, try choosing three or four different areas that you would like to work on that day. Once you have selected them, make a list. Put them in order, starting with the area that you feel you need to focus on the most. You could even date the list, so that you can keep track of the areas you have been working on.

Keeping areas of study listed in order of priority will keep you from always playing the same things when you pick up your guitar. It will also keep you focused on your goals. As you start to get bored with your work in one area, you can refer to your list and know exactly which area to focus on next.

When you finish working on the last area, go back to the first. Continue this cycle until your practice session is over. If you don't get a chance to work on all of your selected areas one day, you may want to pick up where you left off during your next practice session. Make the last area you were working on the first during the next practice session.

Make Practice a Habit

In order to improve quickly, make practice a habit. If possible, practice at the same time each day. This is important for two reasons. The first is that things are easier to start if they are a habit. This is because you don't have to plan to do them. You just do them. For example, you don't have to plan to brush your teeth at night. You just do it. If you can make picking up your guitar each day as automatic as brushing your teeth, you are bound to improve more quickly. The second reason is that if you play at the same time each day, you'll get into a groove where your schedule begins to form around this time. People will begin to know to leave you alone at that time of day.

How to Tell if You're Improving

A good way to gauge your progress is to record yourself playing, write the date on the recording and then put it away for a few months. By making recordings every couple of months, you can listen back and objectively gauge your progress. Improvement comes slowly and it can be hard to tell when or how much you are improving. Ironically, the more you play, the harder it is to tell if you are improving. Just as it can be hard to notice when someone you see every day grows an inch over the course of a year, it can be difficult to notice improvement over less than a few months.

How Much You Need to Practice to be a Pro

Most professional guitarists go through a time when they practice several hours a day. If you would like to make a living playing guitar, plan to practice around twenty hours a week, or more. Around three hours a day is a good goal. Some days you'll have more time to play than others. But, if you want to play professionally, you'll want to make playing and practicing a high priority.

How Much Practice is Too Much

You are practicing too much when other parts of your life start to be neglected. No matter how badly you want to become a great guitarist, you also need to have a life outside of the guitar. Playing the guitar can become an addiction. It can start to control your life instead of being a fun thing to do. Taking a day off every once in a while can actually be good for your playing.

DID YOU KNOW?

In extreme cases, too much practice can even bring on repetitive stress injuries. If you are practicing several hours a day on a regular basis, then you need to be aware of repetitive stress injuries such as *tendonitis*. These injuries are often due to excess tension and strenuous playing without a proper warm-up.

How Often You Should Practice

The more often you practice, the faster you'll improve. Try to pick up your guitar at least once a day, five or six days a week, even if you only play for a few minutes. You'll find that the more you play, the more you want to play.

Eliminating Frustration

As soon as you begin to feel yourself becoming frustrated when practicing, try taking a few slow, deep breaths. This will help relieve frustration and help you concentrate.

Usually, that feeling of frustration comes from trying to learn too much at once. You have "bitten off more than you can chew." When you feel yourself getting frustrated, slow down a little and work on a smaller amount of material (take a smaller bite). Play that smaller piece until you can play it easily, then take another small piece and do the same thing. This will give you the sense of accomplishment that makes it fun to learn new things.

Avoid Negative Thoughts

Sometimes, when you are trying to learn something new and are having difficulty, there will be a negative thought going through the back of your mind saying, "This isn't that difficult, why can't you do this yet, what's the matter with you?" Everyone has this thought at one time or another.

Do your best to ignore this thought, and remember that listening to it will do nothing but add to your frustration. Negative thoughts will make you try to learn things too quickly and may even cause you to believe that you have something learned before you do. This may cause you to move on to something new before you're ready. It takes a conscious effort to ignore these negative thoughts and go ahead and learn at a comfortable, non-frustrating pace.

When you are working on something new, listen for this kind of thought and when you hear it, realize that it is your enemy. When you can do this successfully, learning and practicing will be less frustrating, more fun and more productive.

The Importance of Review

Reviewing what you have learned is an important part of learning to play. Each new thing that you learn builds on what you have learned in the past. Reviewing makes you more able to use the things you've learned by keeping them fresh in your mind. It speeds up the learning process. It will save you from spending time re-learning things. Every month, devote a day or two of practice to review what you've learned in the past few months.

Practice Standing Up

If you are a performer or you would like to be, it is a good idea to make your practice situation as close as possible to an actual performance. If you plan to perform standing up, then you should practice standing up. Playing the guitar can feel a lot different when standing and if your seated position is less than perfect, your hands may be at a different angle than when sitting down.

Why Many Short Practice Sessions are Better than a Few Long Sessions

You can learn more in a short, intense session than you can in a long, unfocused one. Your mind likes to learn things in small bits. When you're learning something new, it helps to learn in short sessions so that you can maintain a high concentration level.

Some days you will have more time to play than others. On days when time is limited, use the time to learn something new. Learn a new scale or chord, or a short, new part of a song. Then use the days when you have more time to polish the things you have learned. Repeat them until they become comfortable for you.

Getting Out Of A Rut

Every player, at one point or another, gets into a rut. We find ourselves playing the same old things each time we pick up the guitar and our playing becomes stale.

The fastest way to get out of a rut is to play even more than usual. Also, try not to play any of your usual songs, licks or riffs for a week. If you tend to often play in one certain key, avoid this key completely for a week and instead play in other, less familiar keys. Each day, make it a point to learn a new song (or even part of one), or a scale or riff. Then record the new thing that you've learned and review what you've recorded the next day. Continue this until you're out of your rut.

Motivation

The best way to get motivated to play is to plan a performance. The performance can be for a few friends or family members, or a larger group of people. The desire to perform well can be extremely inspiring and tends to bring a new focus and sense of urgency to your practicing. This focus can be great for your playing, especially if you feel like your playing is in a rut.

DID YOU KNOW?

After becoming an accomplished "shredder," **Tom Morello** turned his attention to getting new sounds out of the guitar, resulting in his totally unique style. In 1991, he formed Rage Against The Machine, who were among the first to combine metal and hip-hop.

PHOTO • EDWARD G. LINES/COURTESY OF STAR FILE, INC.

A FEW THINGS YOU NEED TO KNOW ABOUT THE MUSIC BIZ

Getting What's Coming to You

How to Copyright a Song You've Written

Once you have written a song and recorded it on tape, you automatically own the *copyright* to that song. This means that you alone have the right to make copies of the song and sell them. In order to protect that right, it is a good idea to have your song registered with the Copyright Office of the Library of Congress. Once your song is registered, you can prove in court that the song is yours (should anyone try to steal it).

To have your song registered, you'll need to visit this Website:

http://www.copyright.gov/

Navigate to "Forms" and download the forms, or go to "Electronic Copyright Office" (eCO), where you can register online.

The Copyright Office contact information, as of this writing, is as follows:

U.S. Copyright Office
101 Independence Ave. S.E.
Washington, D.C. 20559-6000
(202) 707-3000

There is a charge each time you register, but, you can register more than one song at a time. If you register more than one song at a time, the recording you send in will need to have a name, such as "Collection of Songs."

How You Get Paid When Your Song Gets Played on the Radio

Technically, each time your song is played on the radio, on TV or anywhere else considered to be in public, you should be paid a fee. Because it would be impossible for you to keep track of each time your song is played and to collect the fee, there are agencies that do this for you. These agencies are called "performing rights collecting organizations." Their job is to monitor radio stations, TV stations and other places where songs are played for the public and pay you the fee for each time your song is played. The size of this fee depends on where your song is played. A hit song played all over the country can make the writer rich on performance royalties alone. The two main performing rights collecting organizations are ASCAP, which stands for the "American Society of Composers, Authors and Publishers" and BMI, which stands for "Broadcast Music Incorporated." To join either ASCAP or BMI, go to their Websites, or write them a letter requesting an application.

To contact ASCAP, write to: ASCAP, 1 Lincoln Plaza, New York, NY 10023 or see www.ascap.com.

To contact BMI, write to: BMI, 320 West 57th Street New York, NY 10019 or see www.bmi.com.

Why You Don't Have To Pay when Your Band Plays Another Band's Music

Club owners and promoters pay a "blanket fee" to the performing rights collecting organizations. This fee covers all of the performance royalties for the music performed in their venue.

Career Tips

Where You Should Live

To become a pro, it will help to live in or near a major music city. Some cities that are known for their music scene are: New York, NY; Los Angeles, CA; Nashville, TN; and Austin, TX. There are many cases of bands making it out of small towns, but most successful bands are based in cities with thriving music scenes. There are several reasons for this. One is that major music cities have more places for bands to play. Another is that most music industry companies are in major cities.

Networking and How it Can Help Your Career

Networking is the process of making contacts within the music industry. To a certain extent, the old saying, "it's not what you know but who you know" can be true. Who you know can play a large part in your success as a musician. Well-connected people have made a science out of networking. They know that the people who are on their way up are the people who make the best contacts.

Keep an eye out for energetic, ambitious people who are moving up in the industry. These are the people who will end up in high positions later on. You never know where someone will end up. A person interning at a record label could someday be the president of that label. The person who will be the most likely to help your career is a person that you have known for some time. The ideal contact is one who you knew when they were first starting out and have kept in touch with over time.

Getting a Record Contract

There are several different ways to get a record contract. To understand how to get a record contract, it will help to understand how a record company works.

A record company is basically a bank that lends artists money and is paid back through record sales. After the record company *recoups* (makes back all of the money that they spent on recording, promotion and tour support) the remaining money made from record sales is divided between the record company and the band.

The person at the record company that "signs" a band is called an "A&R" person (artists and relations). The A&R people take a big chance when they sign a band because they could end up losing their job if the band is not successful.

One way to get a record contract is to record an album yourself, sell as many copies as possible and build up a following by playing live and promoting your band. A record company is more likely to sign a band that has already proven itself by building up a fan base and selling albums on its own.

Another way to get a record deal is to make a demo of a few of your band's best songs and send it to an A&R person at a record company. If the A&R person hears the demo and thinks your band just may be the next big thing, he or she will want to see the band play live. The catch here is that the A&R person is unlikely to take the time to listen to your demo, unless they have already heard about your band from a trusted source.

The way to get them to listen to your demo is to be recommended by an inside source. For more information on the music business, check out the book *This Business of Music: The Definitive Guide to the Music Industry,* by M. William Krasilovsky, et al.

Performance Contract

Here is a sample contract for a private party or wedding gig. You can use this as a template to create your own contract, adding or subtracting points as necessary. Anywhere you see text underlines, just replace it with your own information.

(Your name, address, phone number, fax number and e-mail address here)

Dear John Doe,

This contract will confirm our engagement to provide music for your wedding reception to be held on June 17 in the year 2010 beginning at 7:00 p.m. We will play the equivalent of 3 sets of 50 minutes each between the hours of 7:00 p.m. and 10:00 p.m. with two short breaks of 10 minutes each, during which we will provide recorded music. Our attire will be suits and our repertoire will consist of see attached list. The band consists of Steven Jones, keyboards; Bill Smith, guitar; John Brown, bass; Thomas Miller, percussion.

As agreed, I will provide the following equipment: all musical equipment, PA system, recorded music during breaks.

You will provide the following equipment: sheltered playing area, electrical power.

Food and drink of the same quality provided to your guests will also be provided for the band [note here whether the band is to be fed free of charge, are subject to a cash bar, etc.]. It is to be made clear to the caterer and/or staff at the venue that the band members are to be treated as your guests. [These items are pertinent mainly if you are playing a gig at which is food is to be served. Note that if your band consists of more than eight people, it may be difficult to get the client to agree to a "free food" arrangement.]

Our fee for this engagement will be $800.00, which includes all transportation costs. To activate this agreement I must receive a nonrefundable deposit of $80.00 by June 3, 2010. The balance is to be paid to me immediately following the engagement. If overtime is required, and if other obligations do not prevent us from continuing our performance, the rate is $150.00 per half hour, or any fragment thereof.

In case of injury or illness, at my sole discretion I reserve the right to replace any member of my group to ensure the quality of performance you have requested. Please make sure that we are advised of any special song requests well in advance. If you have more than one special request, additional rehearsal costs will apply. Also, please make sure to provide us with adequate directions to the engagement at least two (2) weeks in advance.

Please sign and immediately return both copies of this agreement to me along with the deposit. I will countersign and immediately send one copy to you for your files. If the deposit is in the form of a check, please make it payable to Steven Jones.

If you should have any further questions, feel free to contact me via the information above.

Sincerely,
Steven Jones

Accepted by (X) _____ dated February 1, 2010

Address_____

Telephone _____ Email_____

True Stories

Here are a couple of true stories about bands that have gotten signed to major labels.

Dirty Looks

Dirty Looks was a band that played the club circuit and had a few independent albums out on a small record label from France called Axe Killer Records. The band built up a strong following by playing constantly up and down the East Coast. They changed record companies and released an album on Mirror Records, which belonged to the owner of a large music store in Rochester, New York called the "House of Guitars." This album was reviewed in Billboard Magazine and the next day several record companies, including Atlantic Records, contacted them and were interested in hearing the band. The next few months were spent showcasing for different labels and the band eventually decided to sign with Atlantic Records.

FROM LEFT TO RIGHT:
Paul Lidel, the author
Henrik Ostergaard
Gene Barnett
Jack Pyers

PHOTO: RD TOWNSEND (1987)

Dangerous Toys

Dangerous Toys was signed to Columbia Records after a friend sent a tape of the band playing live to a manager she knew in Los Angeles. The tape sat on the manager's desk for two months. When he finally listened to it, he contacted the band immediately and arranged to fly to Austin, Texas to see them play. The band signed a contract with the manager that said the manager had ninety days to get the band a record contract. The manager knew people at Columbia Records and arranged for an A&R person from the label to see the band play live. Soon after this performance, the band was signed to Columbia Records.

CLOCKWISE FROM BOTTOM:
Jason McMaster
Mark Geary
Paul Lidel, the author
Scott Dalhover
Mike Watson

PHOTO: WYATT MCSPADDEN (1994)

PART 4: REFERENCE

CHANGING STRINGS

Fear not! Putting on a new string is not difficult.

A guitar string, especially a light-weight steel string or nylon string, can break if:
- It has been tightened too much
- It has been "bent" too far with the fretting hand
- It has been strummed or plucked too hard
- It has gotten too old
- There is a mechanical fault (sometimes due to wear) with the nut. Your new guitar should not have this problem.

Even if you don't break one, no guitar string is made to last forever. After awhile, your strings will begin to sound dull and lifeless, and if they're really old, they'll become difficult to tune.

The methods for attaching strings to a guitar are as varied as the many types of guitar bridges and tuning pegs.

Removing Strings

No matter what kind of guitar you have, the first thing you'll have to do is remove the old string (or what's left of it!). If your guitar has a *locking tremolo*, start with Step 1. For any other guitar, skip to Step 3.

TIPS

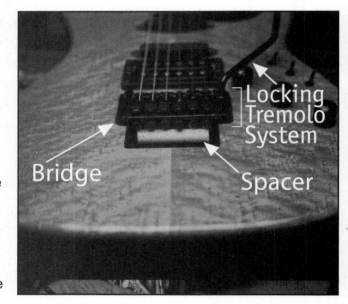

Bridge · Locking Tremolo System · Spacer

Step 1: Release the locking nut.

Step 2: Insert a spacer (see photo to right) between the rear edge of the bridge and the top of the guitar to stabilize the floating motion and make re-tuning easier. Use a piece of wooden doweling or cork.

Step 3: Loosen the string by turning the tuning peg (usually clockwise, but be careful, especially if it's not a broken string) until it is slack. Release the string lock on the bridge saddle (if there is one) and remove the strings. Be careful not to misplace any loose parts.

Attaching New Strings

Putting a string on correctly will help eliminate the biggest source of tuning problems and string breakage: poorly installed strings. Most guitars with conventional tuning pegs can be strung as follows:

Step 1: Insert the string through the appropriate hole in the bridge, guide it over the saddle and nut, then insert it through the hole in the capstan.

If your acoustic guitar has a *push-pin bridge* (plastic or wooden pins secure the ends of the strings to the bridge), gently remove the pin, insert the ball end of your string, and push the pin back into the hole, groove side facing the string.

For attaching strings to a tie-on bridge (classical guitar), see page 166.

Step 2: With your left hand maintaining tension on the string above the nut, and your right hand holding the string halfway down the neck, create enough slack above the fretboard (approx. 3") to allow sufficient winds on the capstan. Use your index finger to gauge the proper distance as you lift the string at about the midpoint of the finger-board. This should allow enough turns around the capstan to securely to hold the string.

Step 3: This will work for most electric and acoustic guitars. **For classical guitars, see page 166.** Secure the string by bringing the loose end over the top of the capstan and then loop it under the portion of string that is going into the hole. Next, bend the string up and back. While maintaining tension on the string with your right hand, wind the string downward around the capstan. Once the string has a bit of tension, you may let go with your right hand.

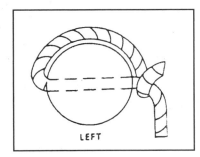

LEFT

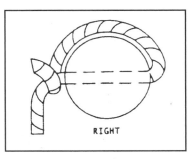

RIGHT

Classical Guitar Tie-On Bridge

Take about 1 to 1½ inches of string, put it through the hole in the tie block, and redirect it back over the block.

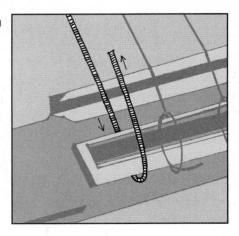

Thread the string underneath itself and back toward the block.

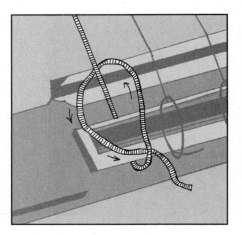

Thread the string through the loop that has been created, trapping the string between itself and the block, then tug on the long end of the string to tighten.

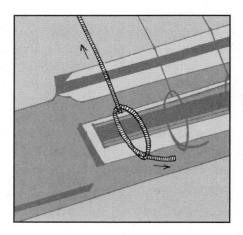

Classical Guitar—Tie-On Tuning Pegs

Thread the string down through the hole in the peg as shown.

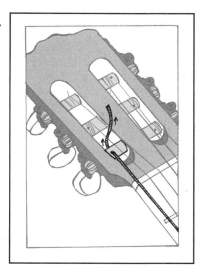

Pull the string back under itself.

Pull the remainder of the string up to secure it, hold it there and turn the tuning peg counterclockwise to tighten.

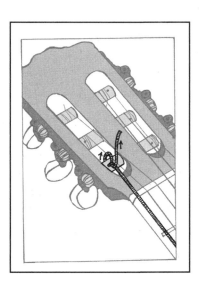

CHORD THEORY

Intervals

Play any note on the guitar, then play a note one fret above it. The distance between these two notes is a **half step.** Play another note followed by a note two frets above it. The distance between these two notes is a **whole step** (two half steps). The distance between any two notes is referred to as an **interval**.

In the example of the C major scale below, the letter names are shown above the notes and the **scale degrees** (numbers) of the notes are written below. Notice that C is the first degree of the scale, D is the second, etc.

The name of an interval is determined by counting the number of scale degrees from one note to the next. For example, an interval of a 3rd, starting on C, would be determined by counting up three scale degrees, or C-D-E (1-2-3). C to E is a 3rd. An interval of a 4th, starting on C, would be determined by counting up four scale degrees, or C-D-E-F (1-2-3-4). C to F is a 4th.

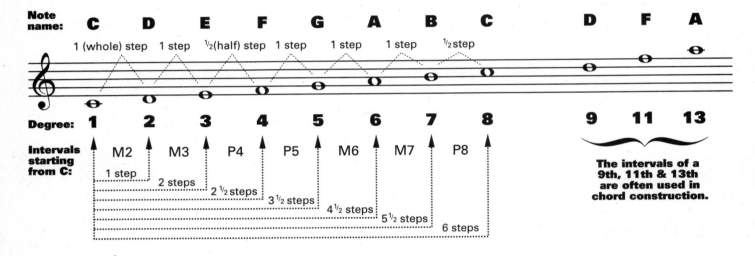

Intervals are not only labeled by the distance between scale degrees, but by the *quality* of the interval. An interval's quality is determined by counting the number of whole steps and half steps between the two notes of an interval. For example, C to E is a 3rd. C to E is also a major third because there are 2 whole steps between C and E. Likewise, C to E♭ is a 3rd. C to E♭ is also a minor third because there are 1½ steps between C and E♭. There are five qualities used to describe intervals: *major, minor, perfect, diminished,* and *augmented.*

    M = Major   o = Diminished (dim)
    m = Minor   + = Augmented (aug)
    P = Perfect

Particular intervals are associated with certain qualities:

2nds, 9ths	=	Major, Minor & Augmented
3rds, 6ths, 13ths	=	Major, Minor, Augmented & Diminished
4ths, 5ths, 11ths	=	Perfect, Augmented & Diminished
7ths	=	Major, Minor & Diminished

When a **major** interval is made *smaller* by a half step it becomes a **minor** interval.

When a **minor** interval is made *larger* by a half step it becomes a **major** interval.

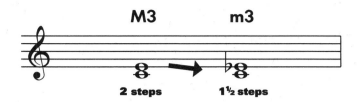

When a **minor** or **perfect** interval is made *smaller* by a half step it becomes a **diminished** interval.

When a **major** or **perfect** interval is made *larger* by a half step it becomes an **augmented** interval.

Below is a table of intervals starting on the note C. Notice that some intervals are labeled enharmonic, which means that they are written differently but sound the same (see **aug2** & **m3**).

TABLE OF INTERVALS

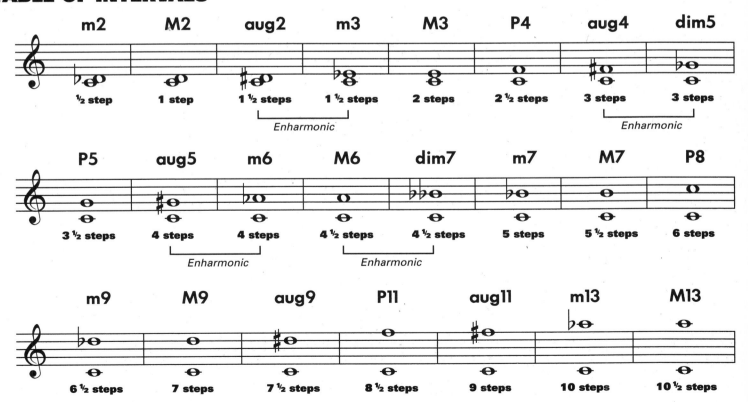

BASIC TRIADS

Two or more notes played together is called a **chord**. Most commonly, a chord will consist of three or more notes. A three-note chord is called a **triad**. The **root** of a triad (or any other chord) is the note from which a chord is constructed. The relationship of the intervals from the root to the other notes of a chord determines the chord **type**. Triads are most frequently identified as one of four chord types: **major**, **minor**, **diminished** and **augmented**.

All chord types can be identified by the intervals used to create the chord. For example, the C major triad is built beginning with C as the root, adding a major 3rd (E) and adding a perfect 5th (G). All major triads contain a root, M3 and P5.

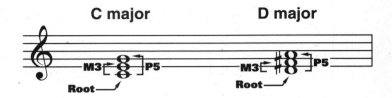

Minor triads contain a root, minor 3rd and perfect 5th. (An easier way to build a minor triad is to simply lower the 3rd of a major triad.) All minor triads contain a root, m3 and P5.

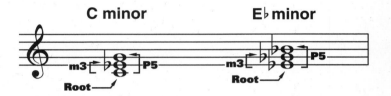

Diminished triads contain a root, minor 3rd and diminished 5th. If the perfect 5th of a minor triad is made smaller by a half step (to become a diminished 5th), the result is a diminished triad. All diminished triads contain a root, m3 and dim5.

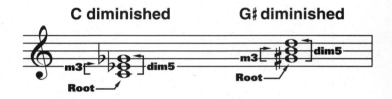

Augmented triads contain a root, major 3rd and augmented 5th. If the perfect 5th of a major triad is made larger by a half step (to become an augmented 5th), the result is an augmented triad. All augmented triads contain a root, M3 and aug5.

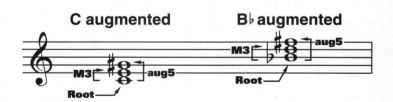

DID YOU KNOW?

An important concept to remember about chords is that the bottom note of a chord will not always be the root. If the root of a triad, for instance, is moved above the 5th so that the 3rd is the bottom note of the chord, it is said to be in the **first inversion**. If the root and 3rd are moved above the 5th, the chord is in the **second inversion**. The number of inversions that a chord can have is related to the number of notes in the chord: a three-note chord can have two inversions, a four-note chord can have three inversions, etc.

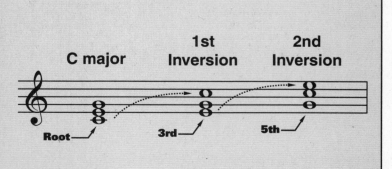

BUILDING CHORDS

By using the four chord types as basic building blocks, it is possible to create a variety of chords by adding 6ths, 7ths, 9ths, 11ths, etc. The following are examples of some of the many variations.

* The **suspended fourth** chord does not contain a third. An assumption is made that the 4th degree of the chord will harmonically be inclined to **resolve** to the 3rd degree. In other words, the 4th is **suspended** until it moves to the 3rd.

Up until now, the examples have shown intervals and chord construction based on C. Until you are familiar with all the chords, the C chord examples on the previous page can serve as a reference guide when building chords based on other notes: For instance, locate C7(♭9). To construct a G7(♭9) chord, first determine what intervals are contained in C7(♭9), then follow the steps outlined below.

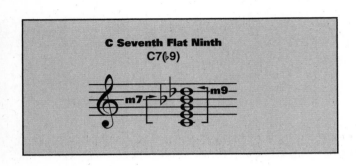

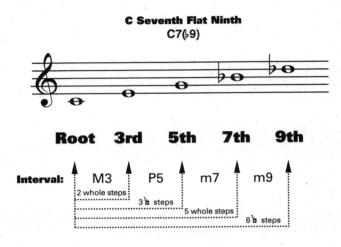

TIPS

- Determine the **root** of the chord. A chord is always named for its root—in this case, G is the root of G7(♭9).

- Count **letter names** up from the **letter name of the root** (G), as we did when building intervals on page 169, to determine the intervals of the chord. Counting three letter names up from G to B (G-A-B, 1-2-3) is a 3rd, G to D (G-A-B-C-D) is a 5th, G to F is a 7th, and G to A is a 9th.

- Determine the **quality** of the intervals by counting whole steps and half steps up from the root; G to B (2 whole steps) is a major 3rd, G to D (3½ steps) is a perfect 5th, G to F (5 whole steps) is a minor 7th, and G to A♭ (6½ steps) is a minor 9th.

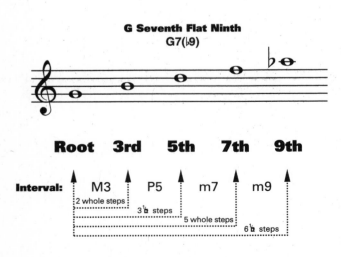

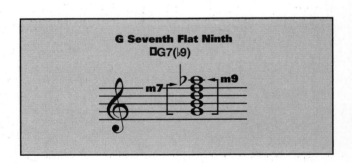

Follow this general guideline to figure out the notes of any chord. As interval and chord construction become more familiar, it will become possible to create your own original fingerings on the guitar. Feel free to experiment!

THE CIRCLE OF FIFTHS

The **circle of fifths** will help to clarify which chords are enharmonic equivalents (notice that **chords** can be written enharmonically as well as **notes**). The circle of fifths also serves as a quick reference guide to the relationship of the keys and how key signatures can be figured out. Clockwise movement (up a P5) provides all of the sharp keys by adding one sharp to the key signature. Counter-clockwise (down a P5) provides the flat keys by adding one flat.

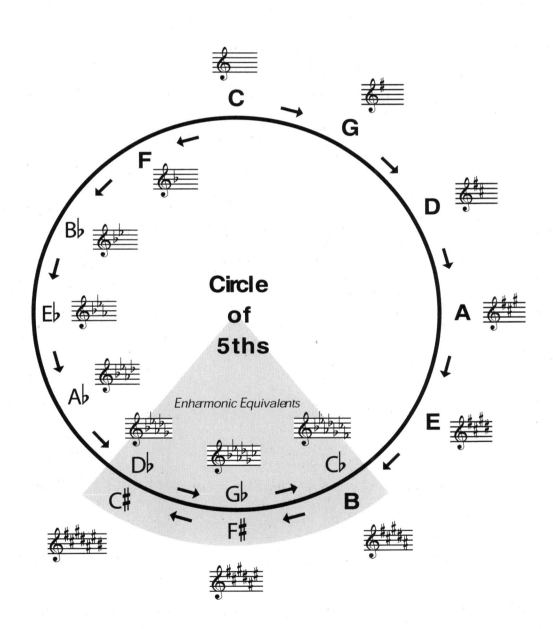

CHORD SYMBOL VARIATIONS

Chord symbols are a form of musical shorthand that give the guitarist as much information about a chord as quickly as possible. Since chord symbols are not universally standardized, they are often written in many different ways—some are understandable, others are confusing. To illustrate this point, below is a listing of some of the ways copyists, composers and arrangers have created variations on the more common chord symbols.

C	Csus	C(♭5)	C(add9)	C5	Cm
C major	Csus4	C-5	C(9)	C(no3)	Cmin
Cmaj	C(addF)	C(5-)	C(add2)	C(omit3)	Cmi
CM	C4	C(♯4)	C(+9)		C-
			C(+D)		

C+	C°	C6	C6/9	Cm6/9	Cm6
C+5	Cdim	Cmaj6	C6(add9)	C-6/9	C-6
Caug	Cdim7	C(addA)	C6(addD)	Cm6(+9)	Cm(addA)
Caug5	C7dim	C(A)	C9(no7)	Cm6(add9)	Cm(+6)
C(♯5)			C9/6	Cm6(+D)	

C7	C7sus	Cm7	Cm7(♭5)	C7+	C7(♭5)
C(addB♭)	C7sus4	Cmi7	Cmi7-5	C7+5	C7-5
C7̶	Csus7	Cmin7	C-7(5-)	C7aug	C7(5-)
C(-7)	C7(+4)	C-7	Cø	C7aug5	C7̶-5
C(+7)		C7mi	C ½dim	C7(♯5)	C7(♯4)

Cmaj7	Cmaj7(♭5)	Cm(maj7)	C7(♭9)	C7(♯9)	C7+(♭9)
Cma7	Cmaj7(-5)	C-maj7	C7(-9)	C7(+9)	Caug7-9
C7̶	C7̶(-5)	C-7̶	C9♭	C9♯	C+7(♭9)
CΔ	CΔ(♭5)	Cmi7̶	C9-	C9+	C+9♭
CΔ7					C7+(-9)

Cm9	C9	C9+	C9(♭5)	Cmaj9	C9(♯11)
Cm7(9)	$C7^9$	C9(+5)	C9(-5)	C7̶(9)	C9(+11)
Cm7(+9)	C7add9	Caug9	$C7^9_{-5}$	C7̶(+9)	C(♯11)
C-9	C7(addD)	C(♯9♯5)	C9(5♭)	C9(maj7)	C11+
Cmi7(9+)	C7(+9)	C+9		C9̶	C11♯

Cm9(maj7)	C11	Cm11	C13	C13(♭9)	C13(♭9♭5)
C-9(♯7)	C9(11)	C-11	C9addA	C13(-9)	C13(-9-5)
C(-9)7̶	C9addF	Cm(♭11)	C9(6)	$C♭13_9$	C(♭9♭5)addA
Cmi9(♯7)	C9+11	$Cmi7^{11}_9$	C7addA	C(♭9)addA	
	$C7^9_{11}$	$C-7(^9_{11})$	C7+A		

READING CHORDS

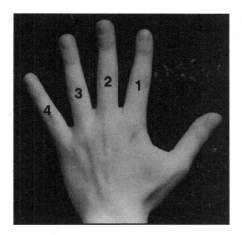

Guitar chord frames are diagrams that contain all the information necessary to play a particular chord. The fingerings, note names and position of the chord on the neck are all provided on the chord frame (see below). The photo at the left shows which finger number corresponds to which finger.

Choose chord positions that require the least motion from one chord to the next; select fingerings that are in approximately the same location on the guitar neck. This will provide smoother and more comfortable transitions between chords in a progression.

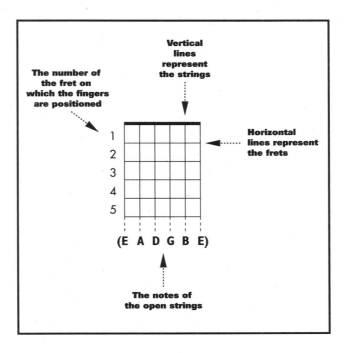

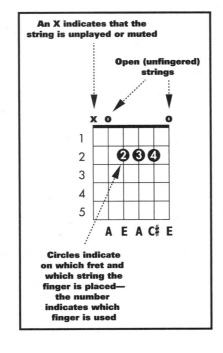

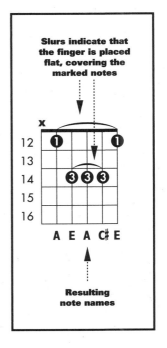

A

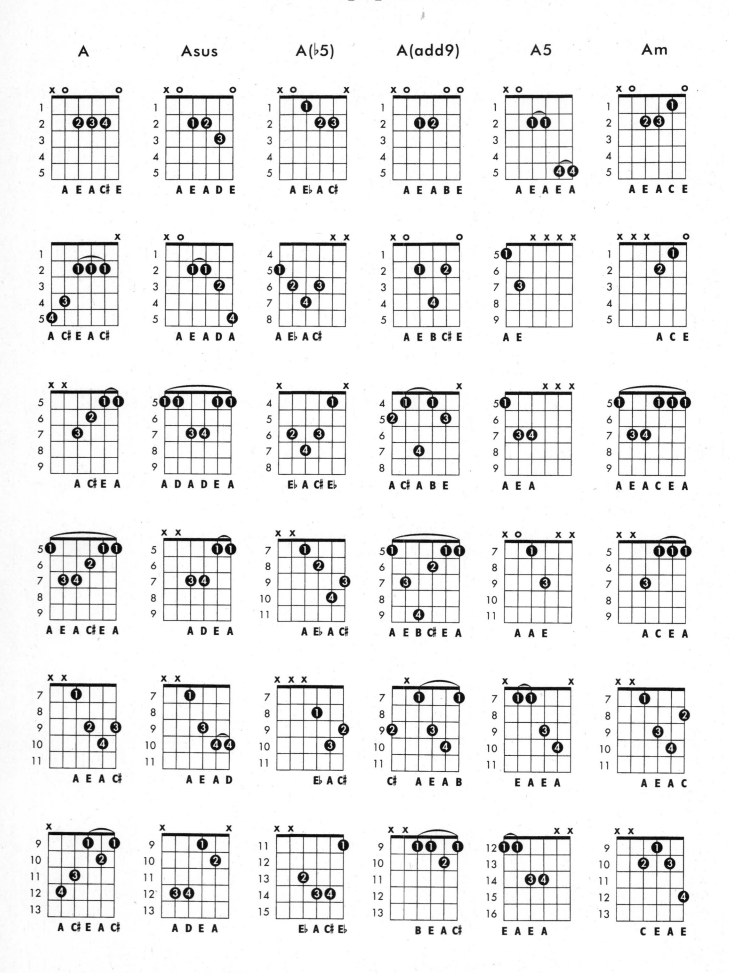

A

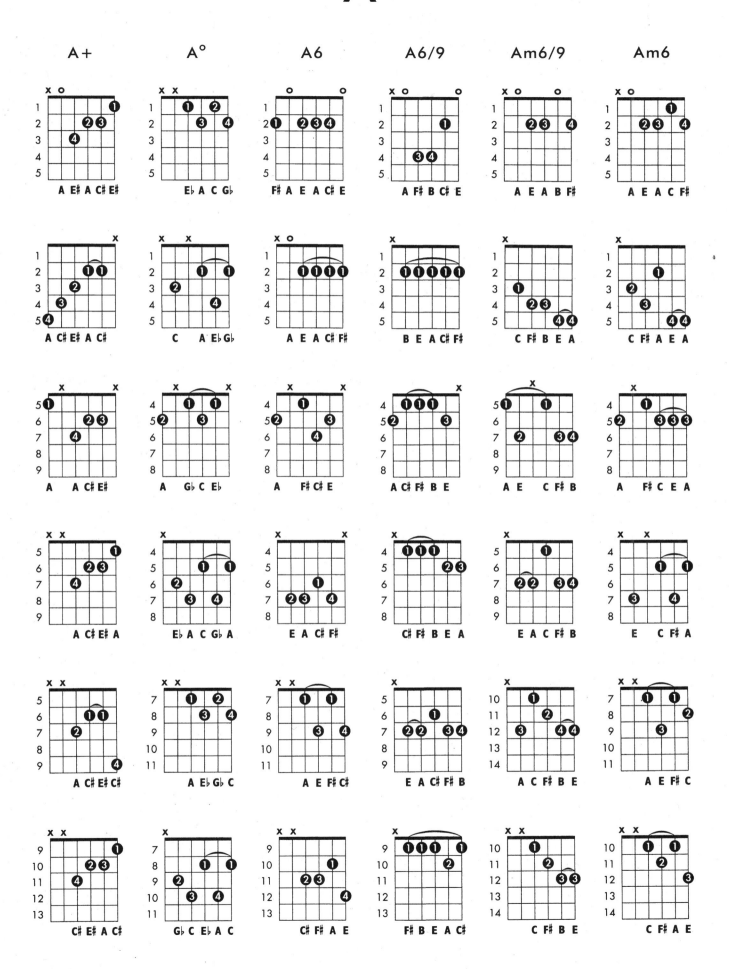

A

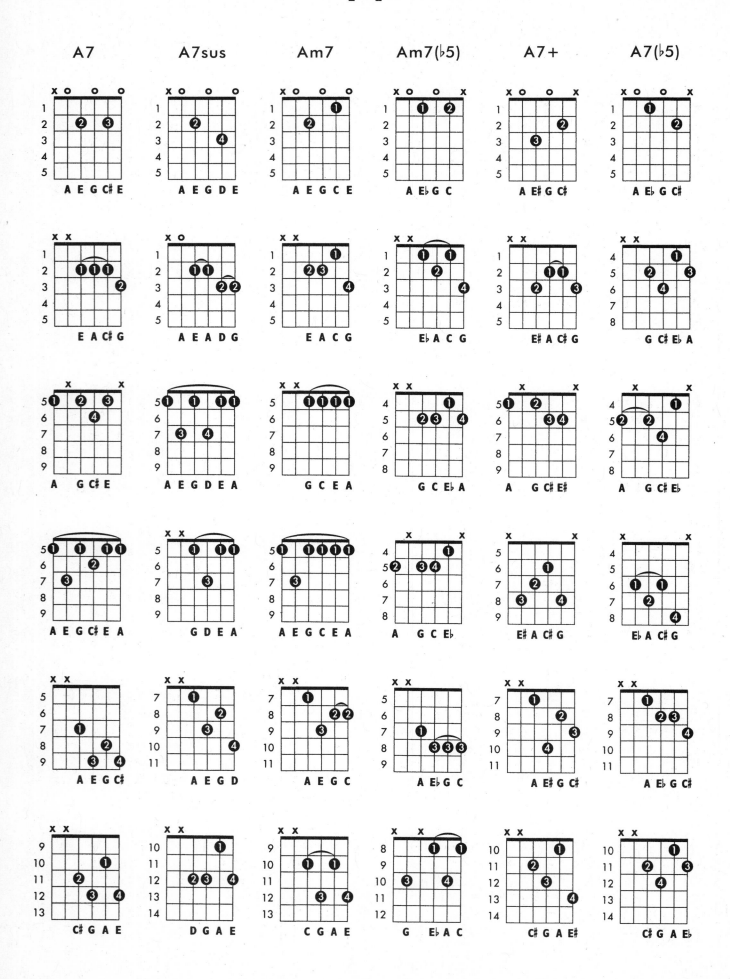

A

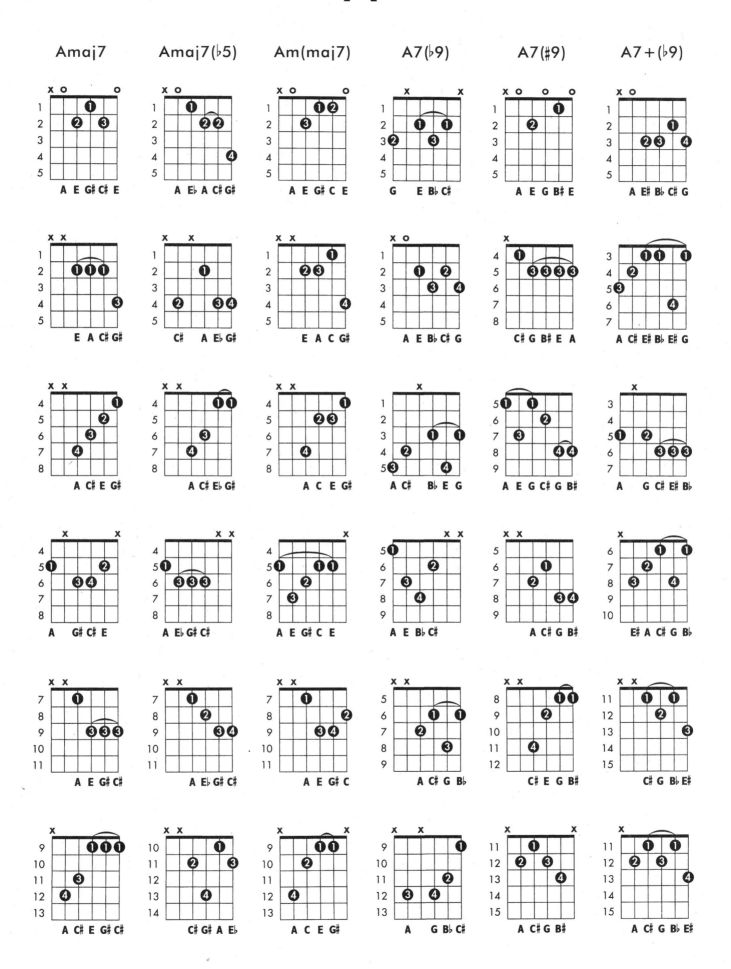

B♭

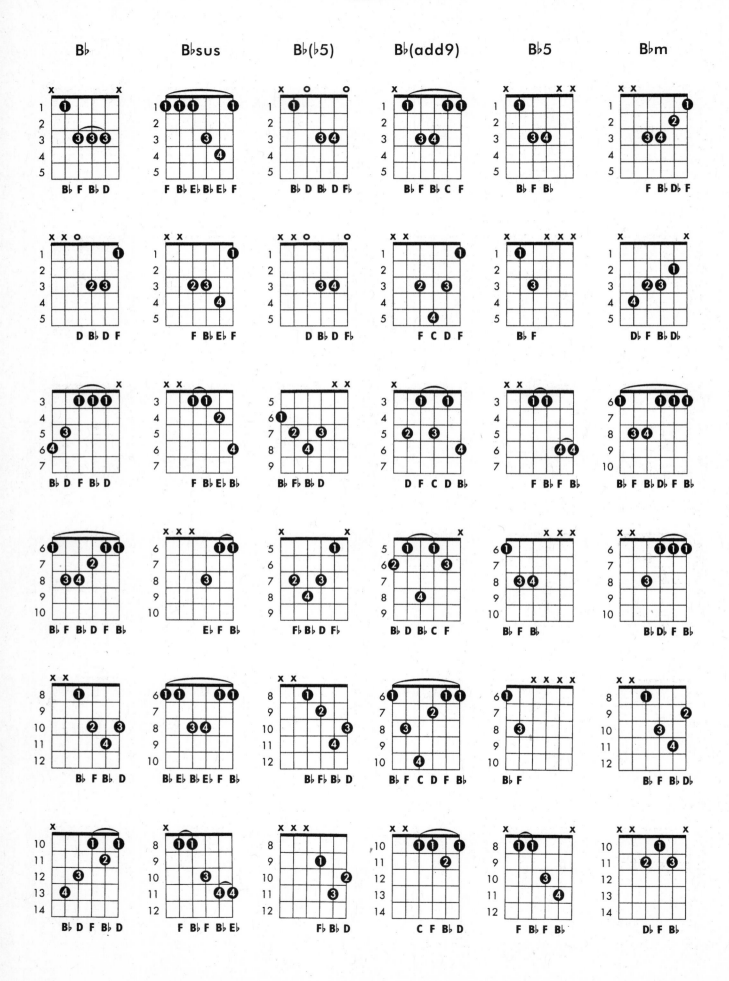

B♭

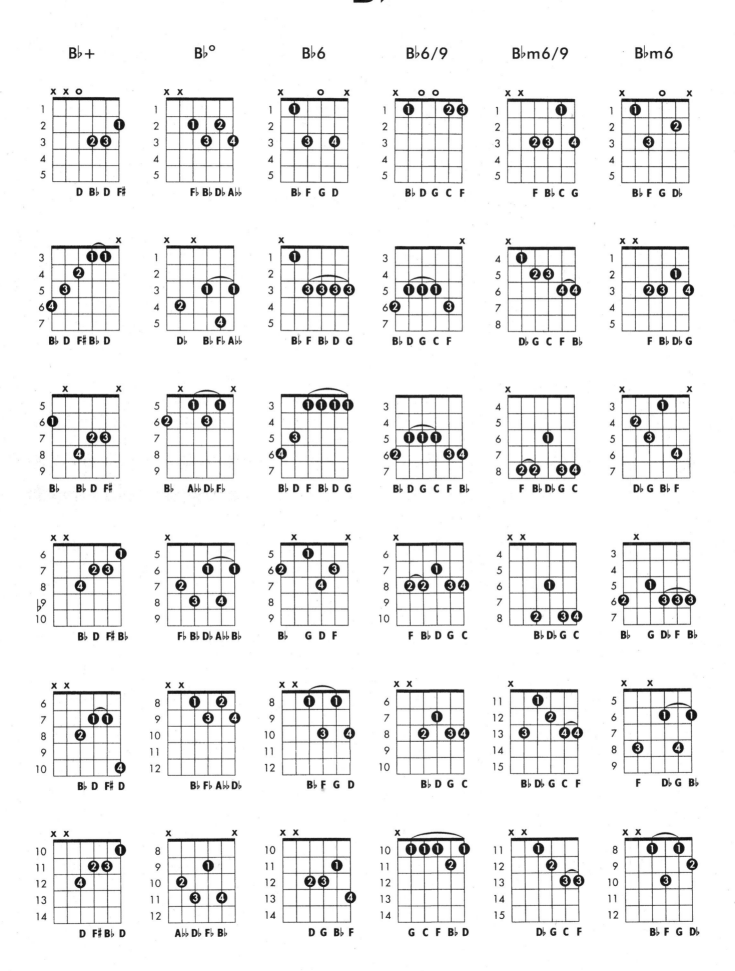

B♭

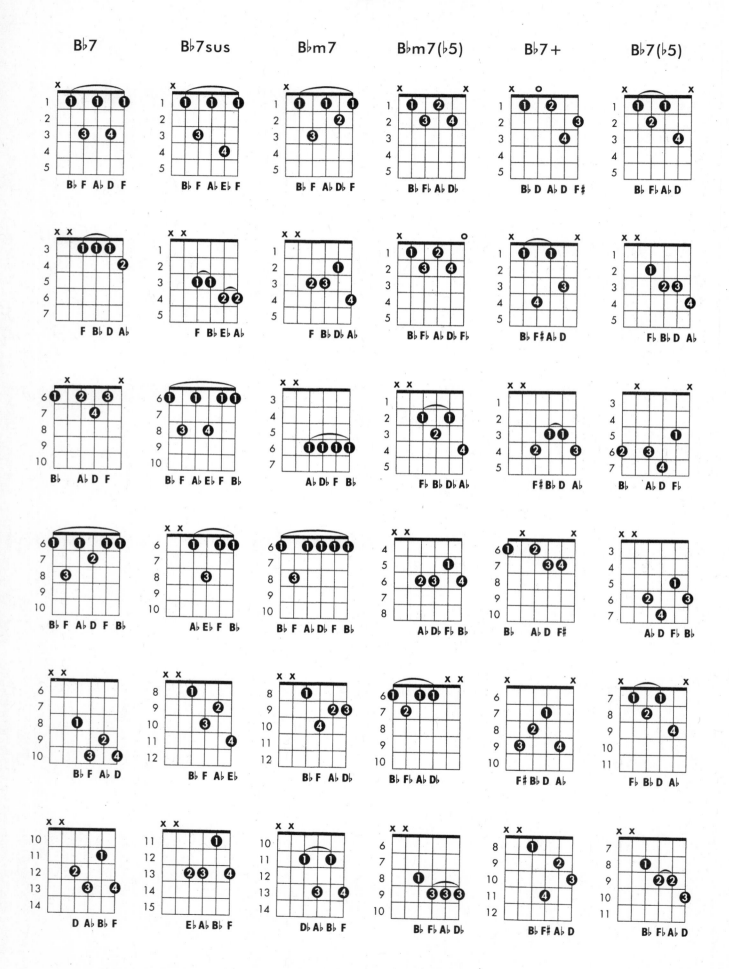

B♭

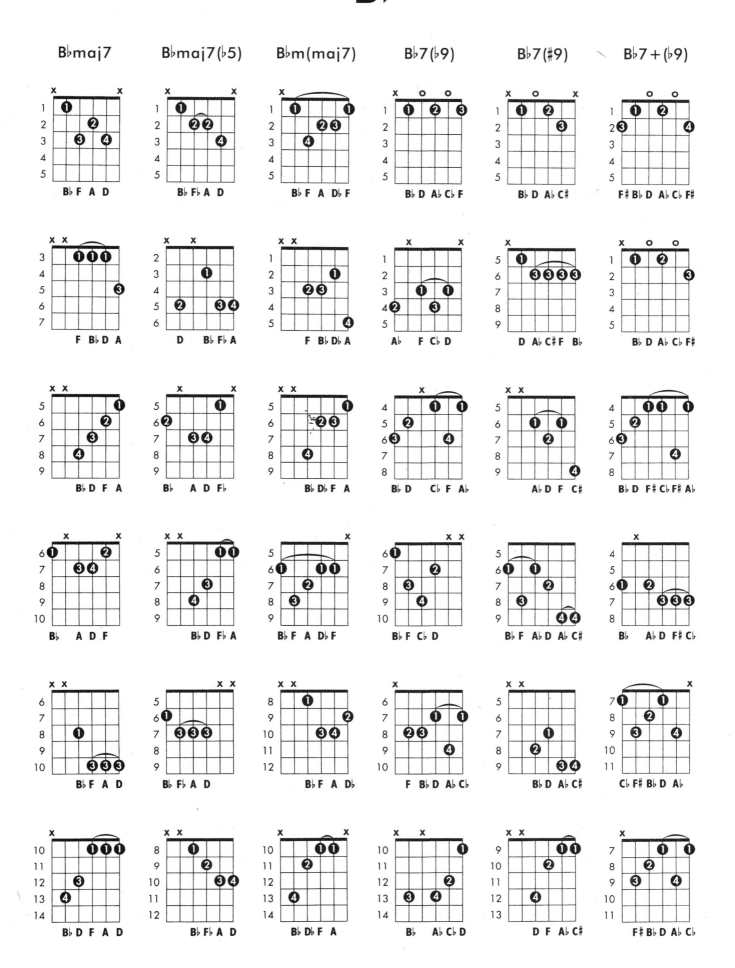

B

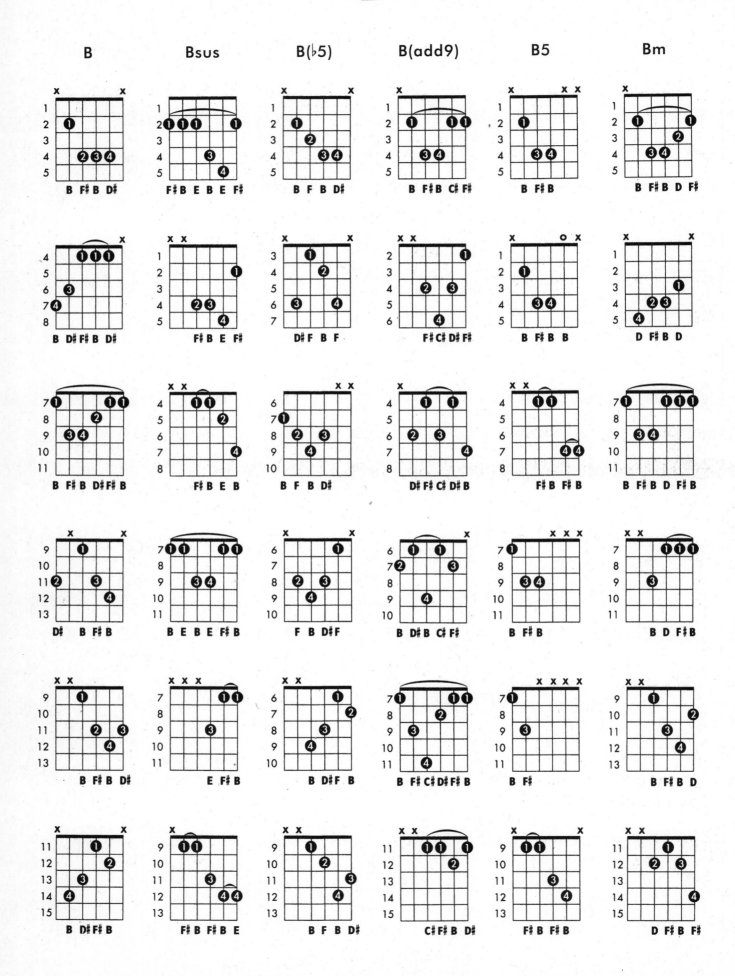

B

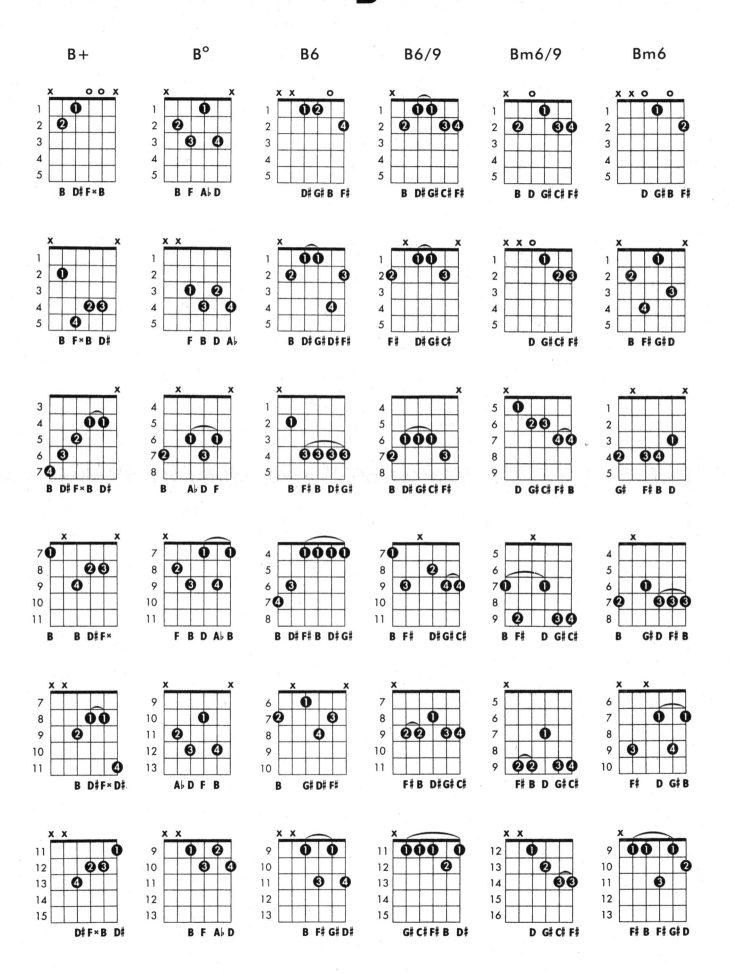

B

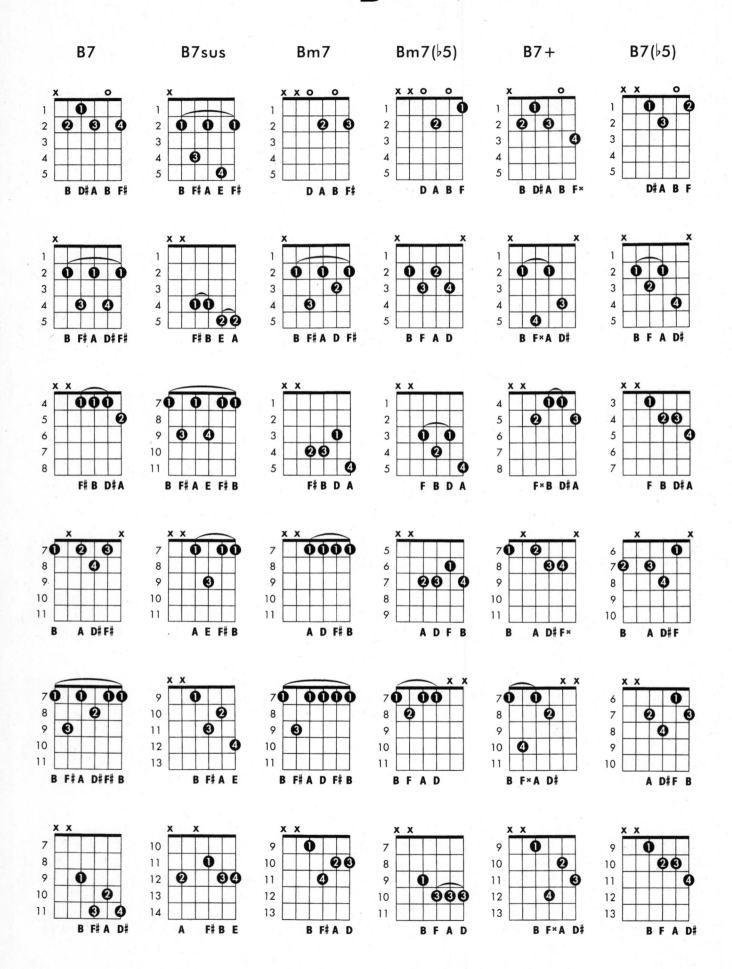

B7 B7sus Bm7 Bm7(♭5) B7+ B7(♭5)

B

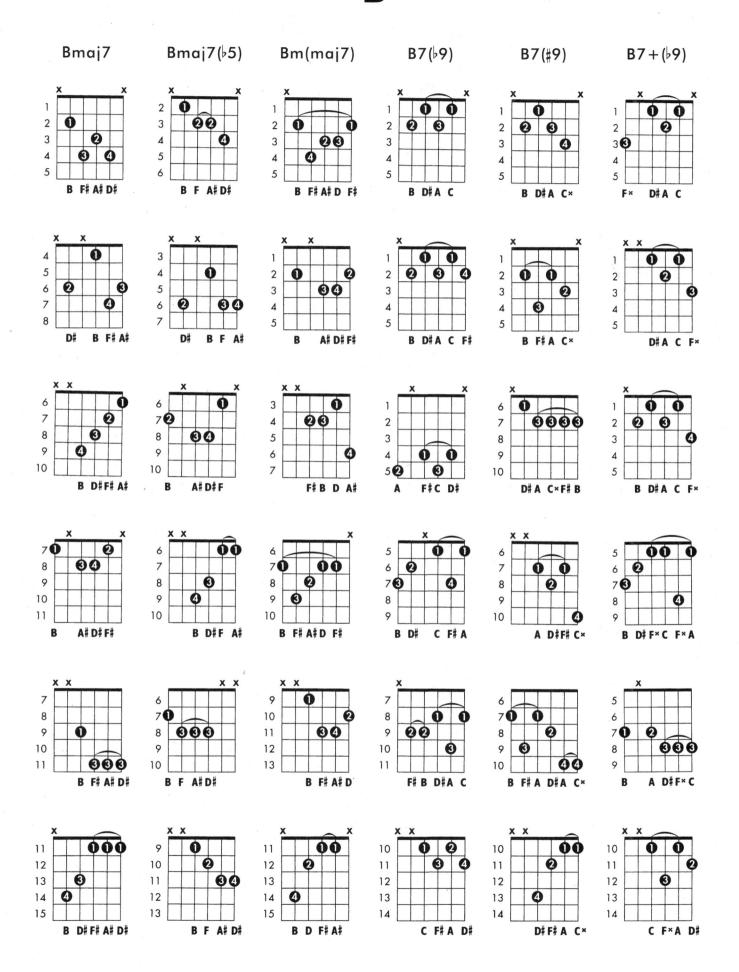

C

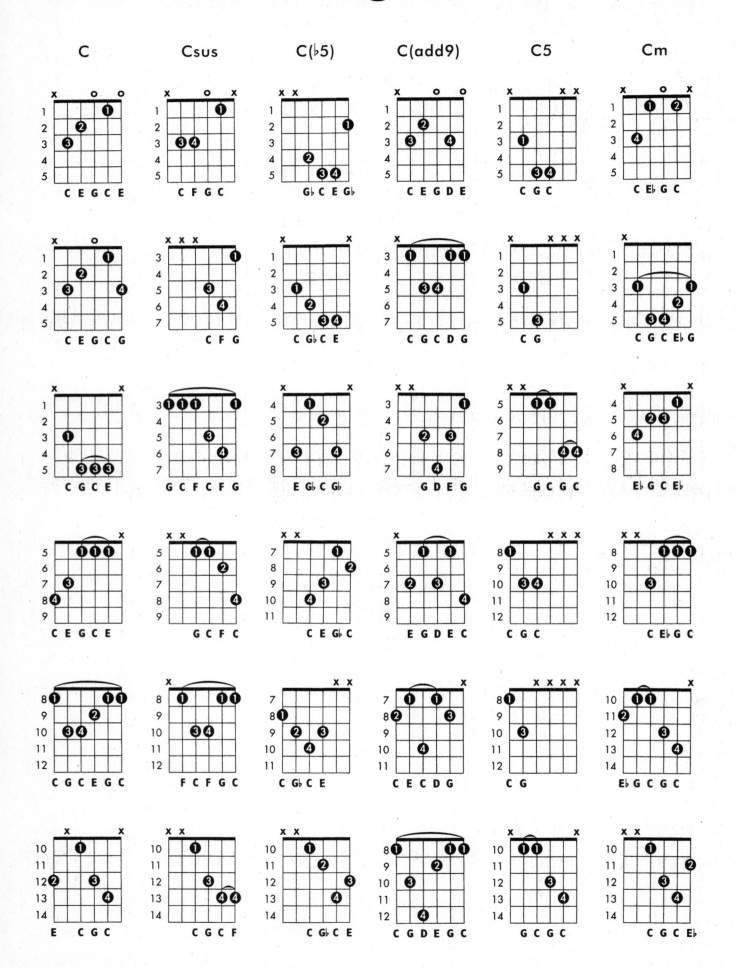

C

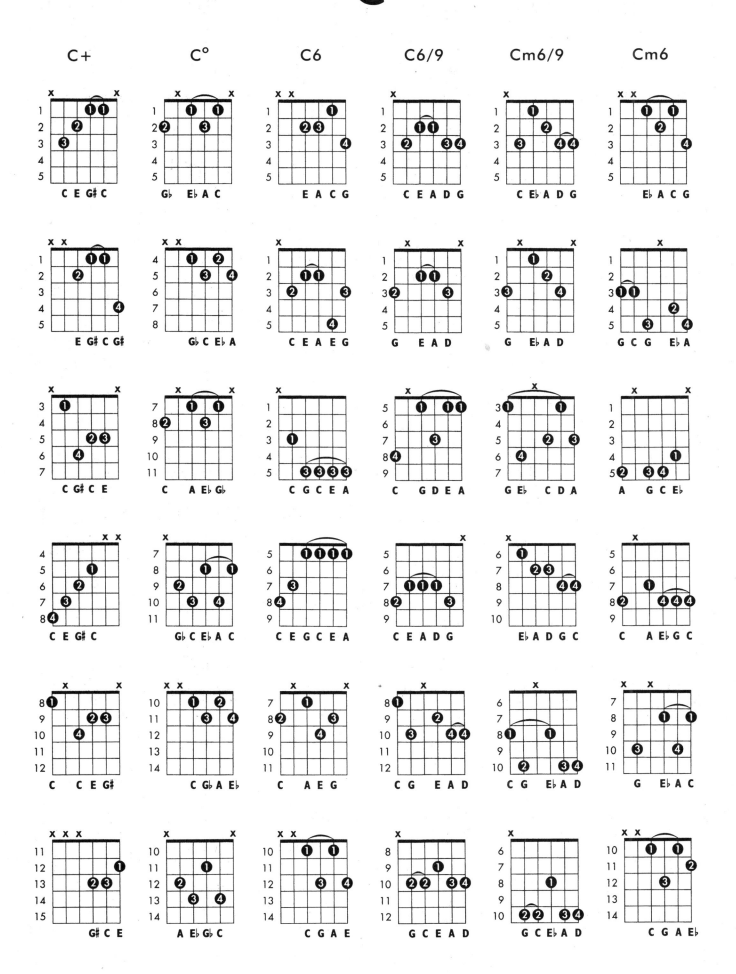

C

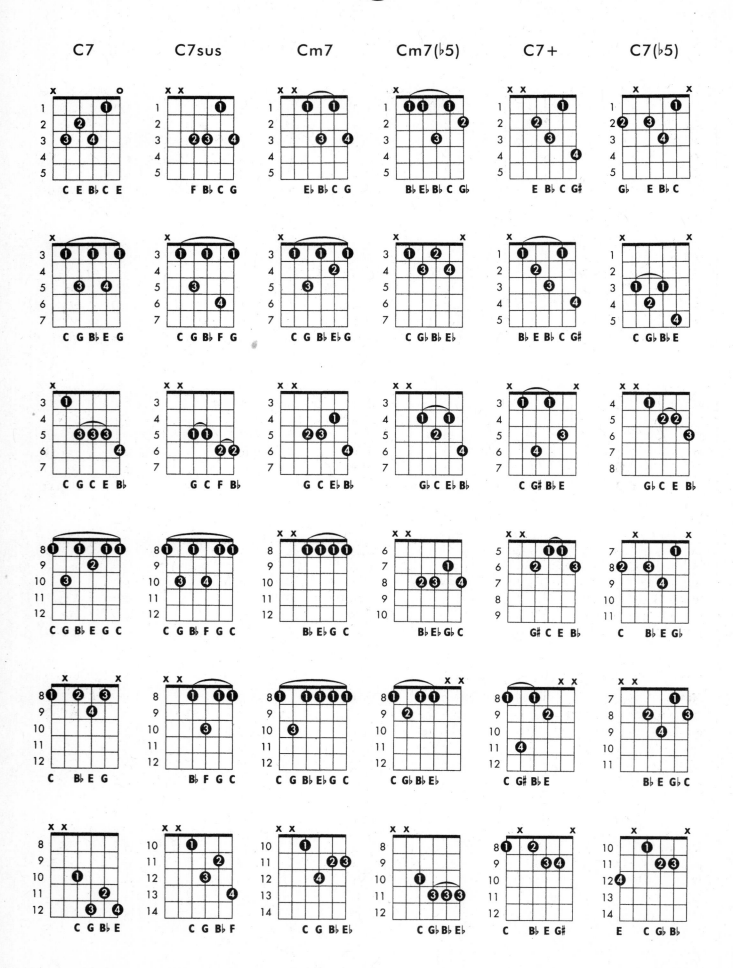

C

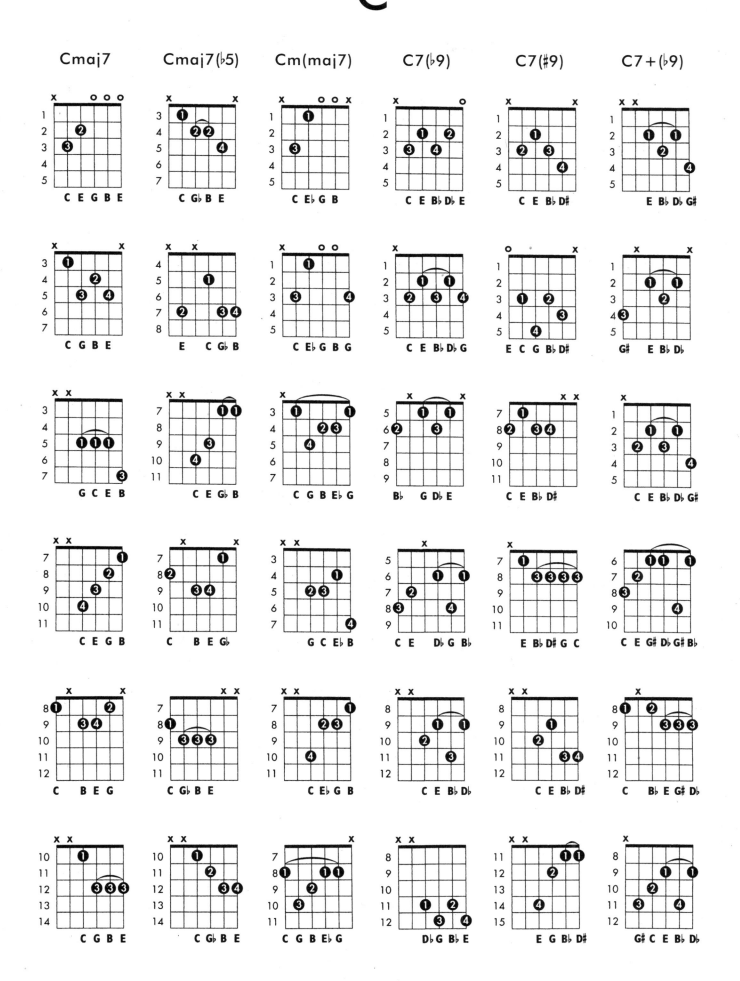

D♭

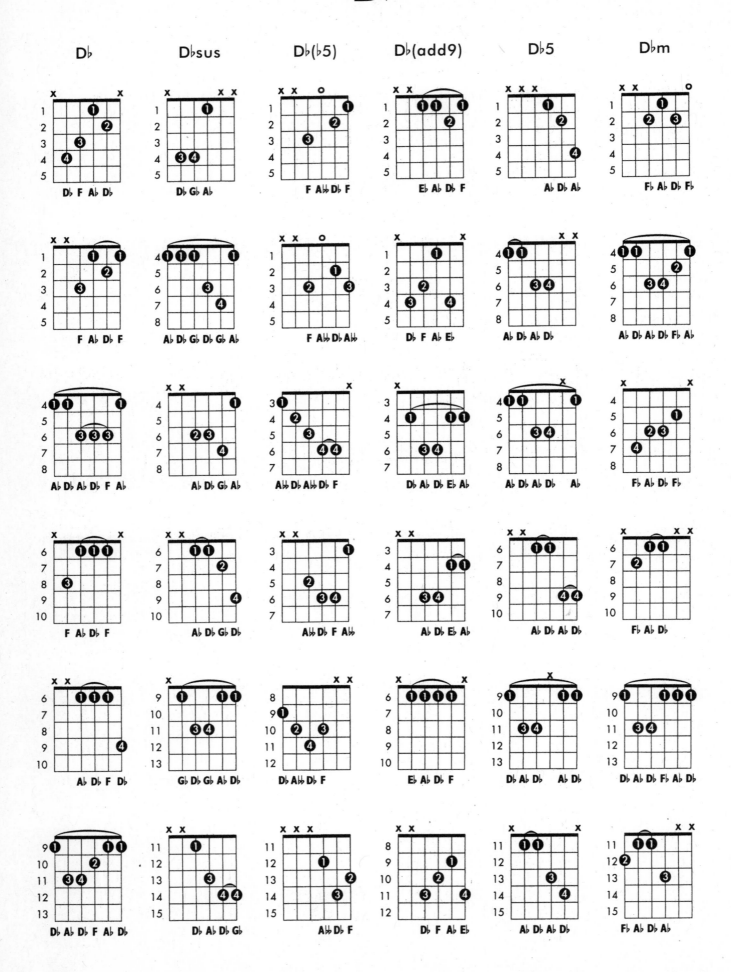

D♭

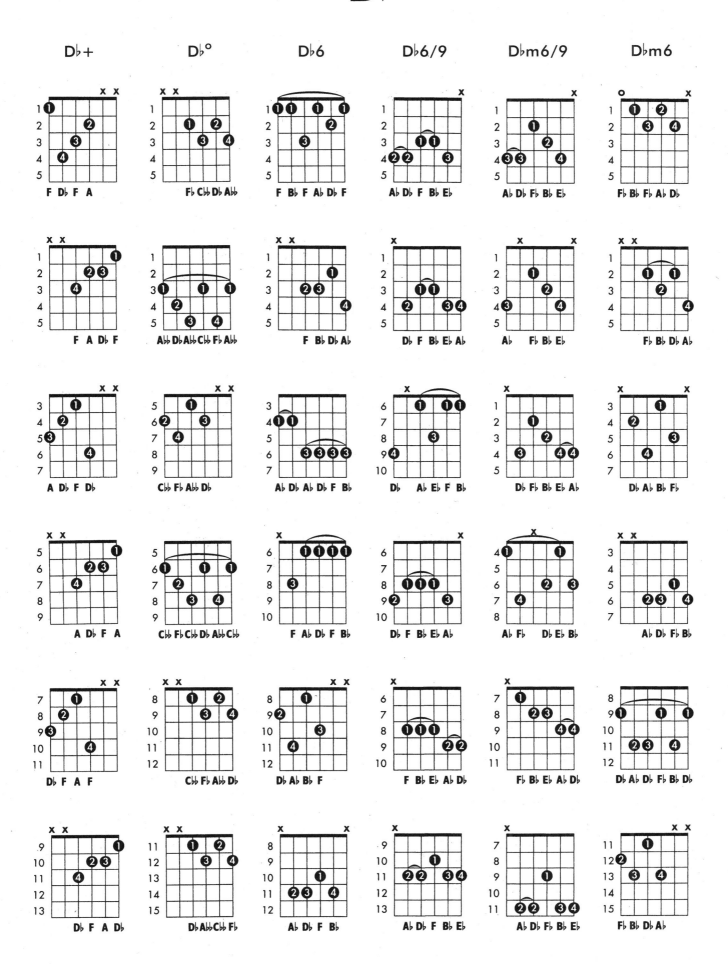

D♭

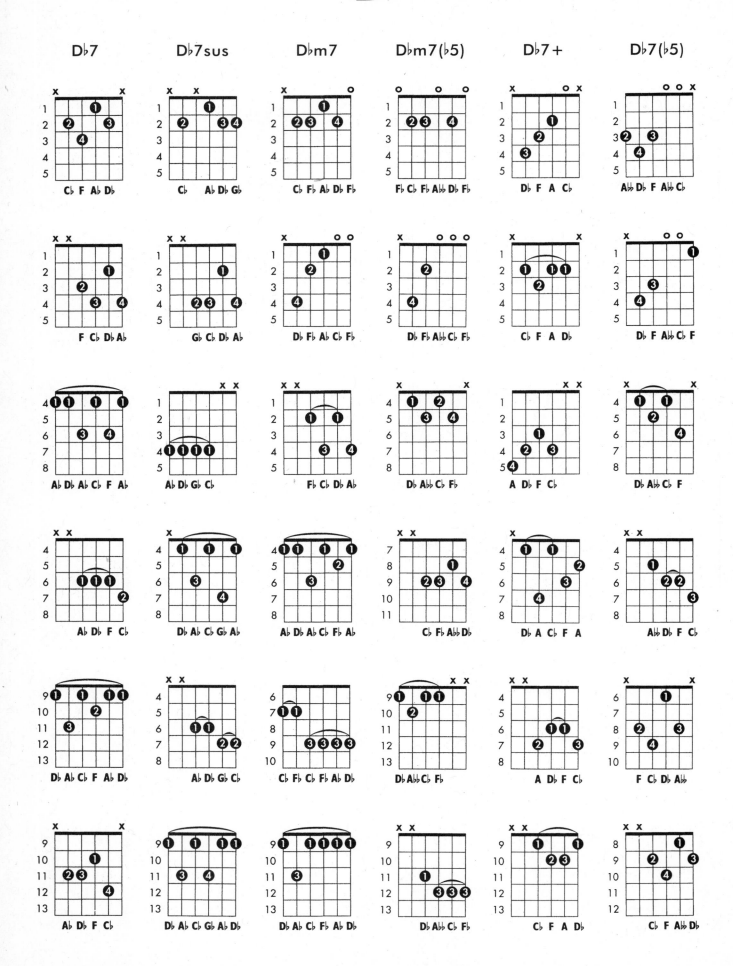

D♭

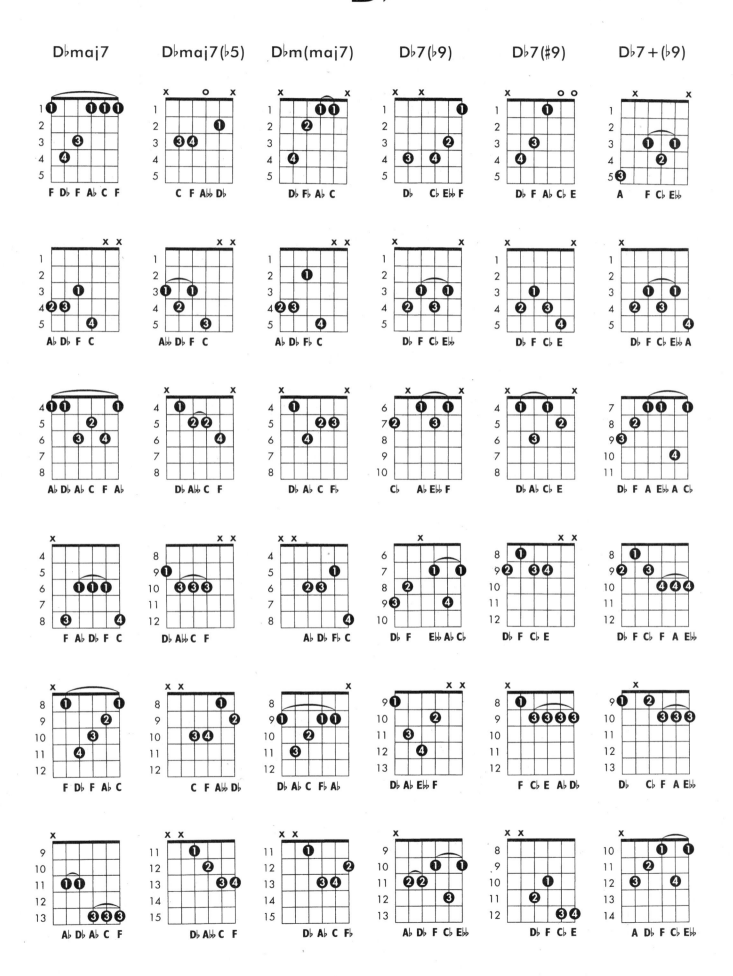

D

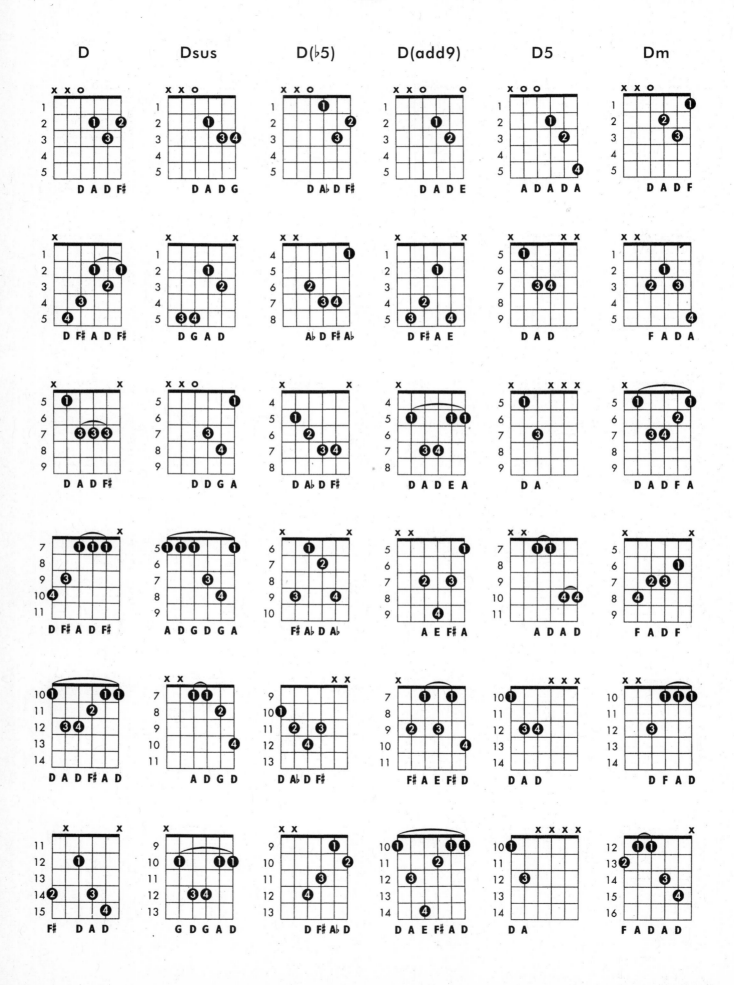

D

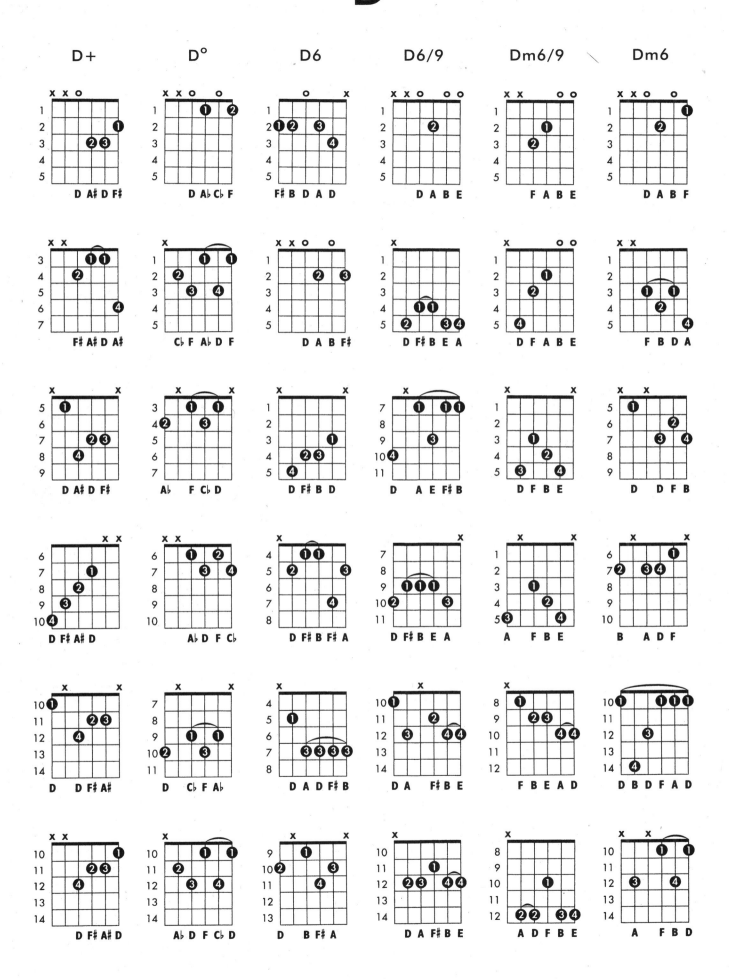

D

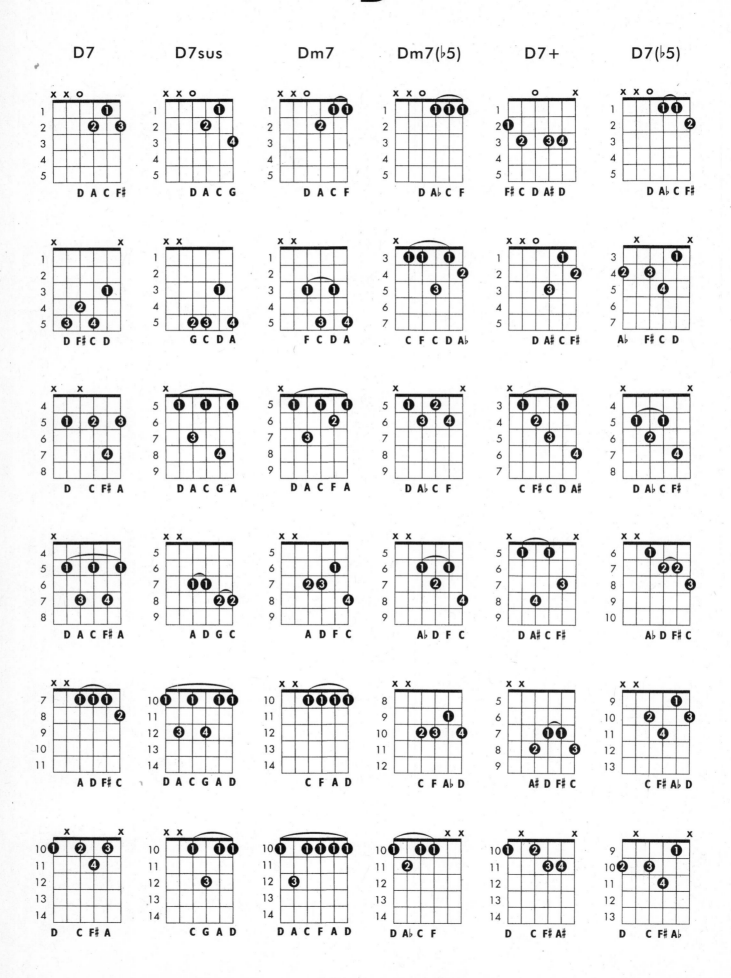

D

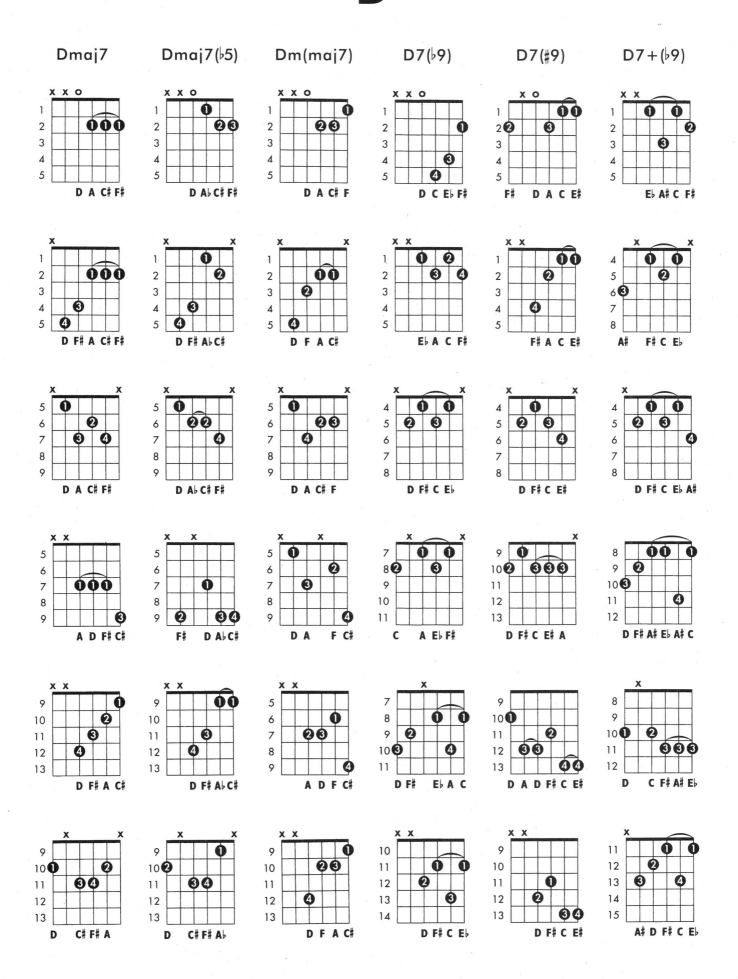

E♭

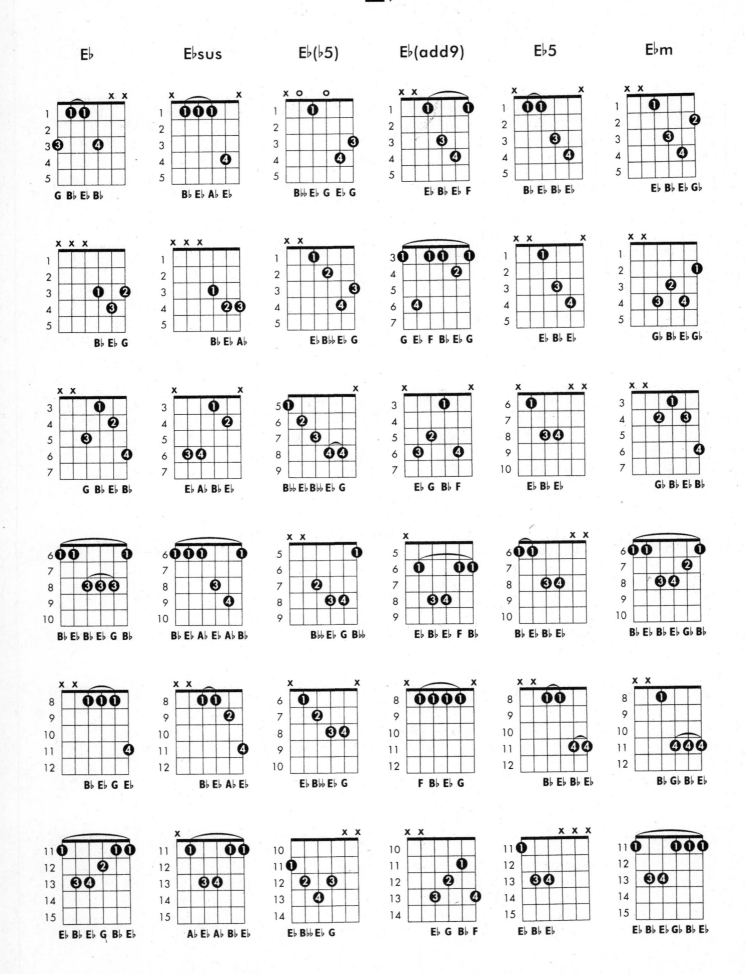

E♭

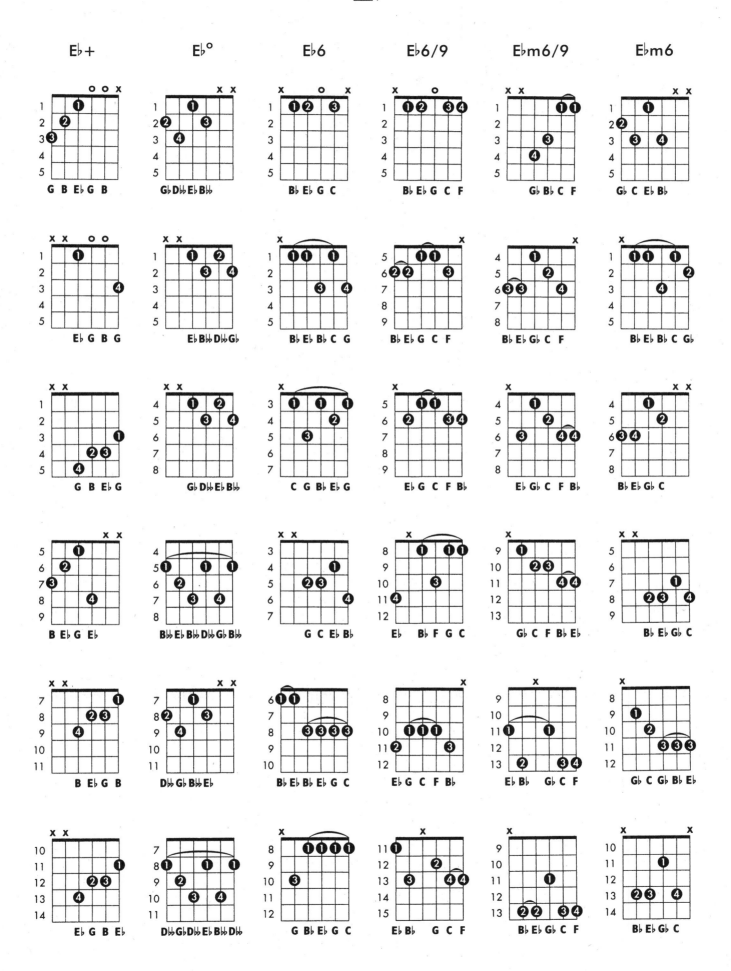

E♭

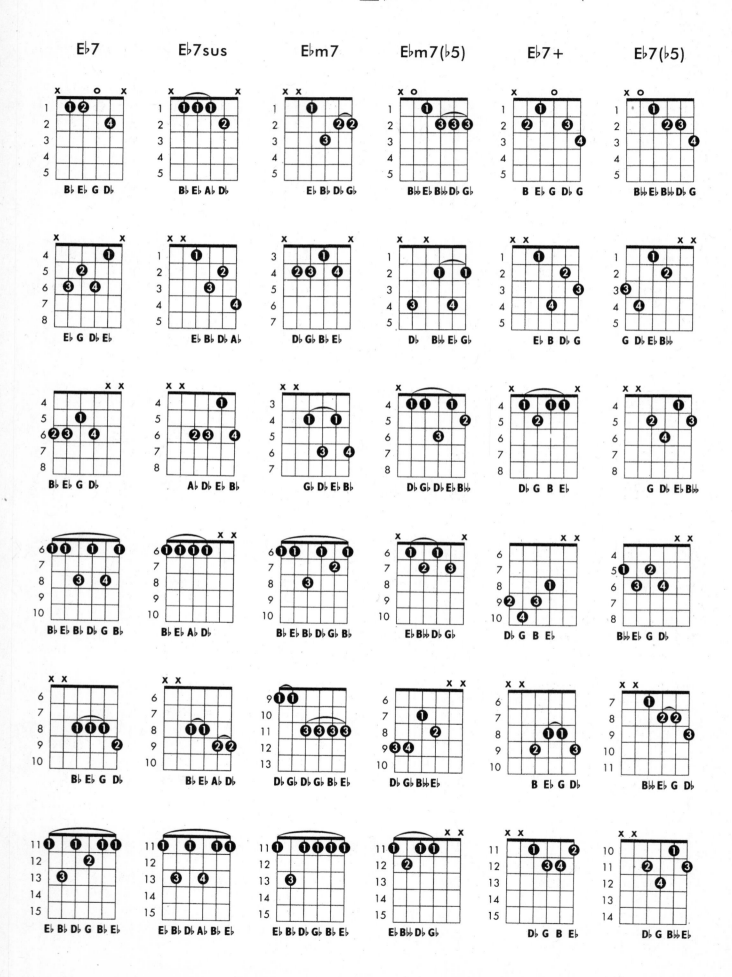

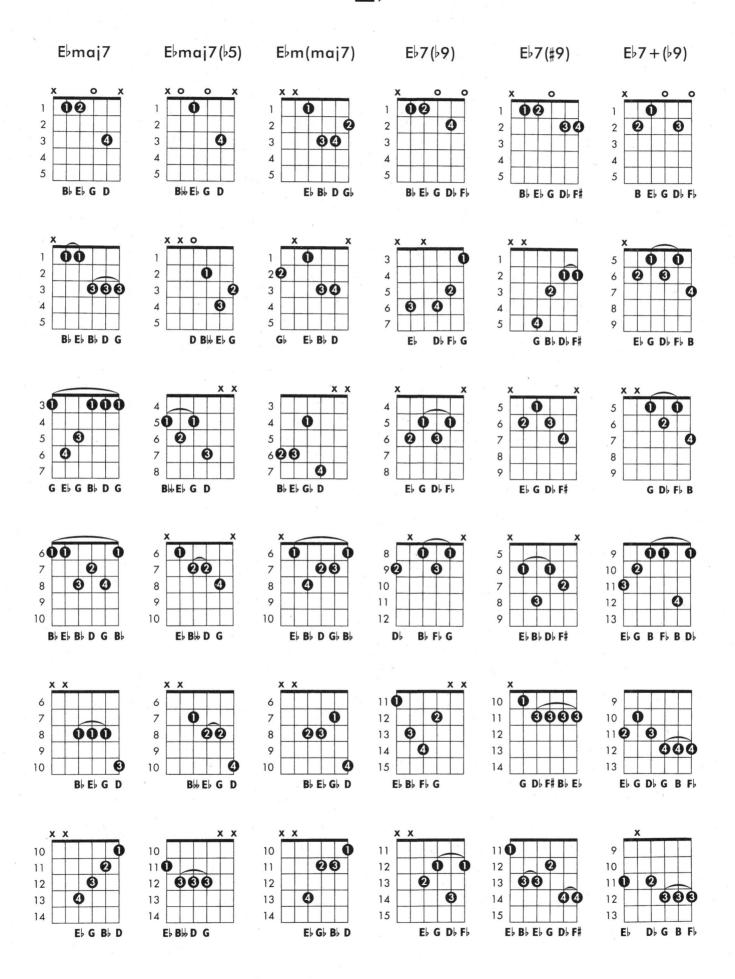

E♭

E

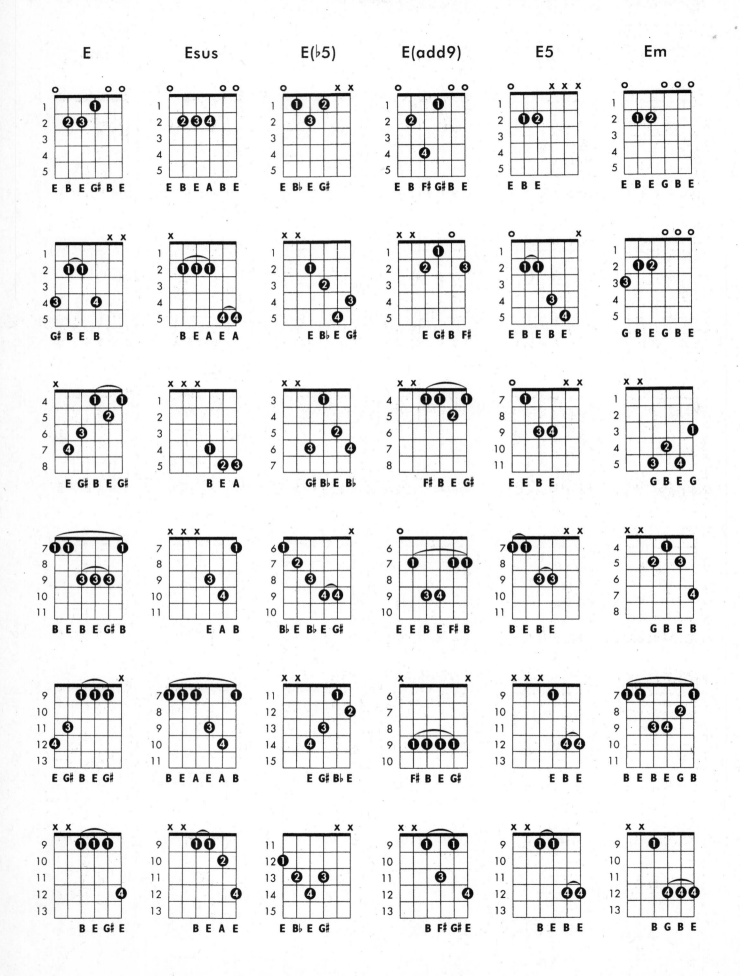

E

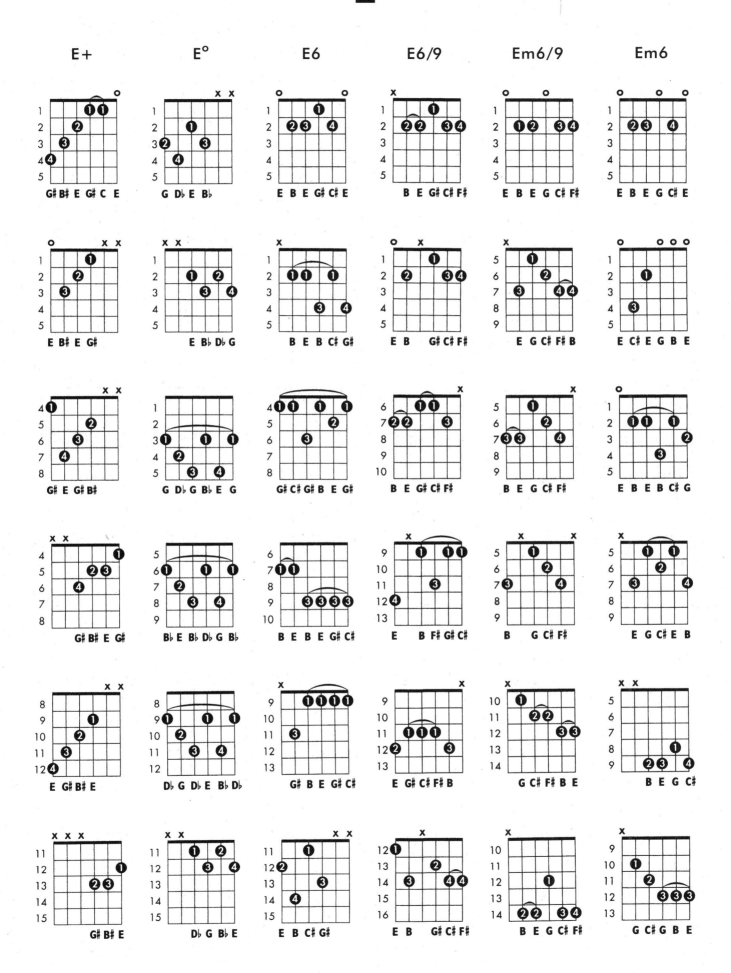

E

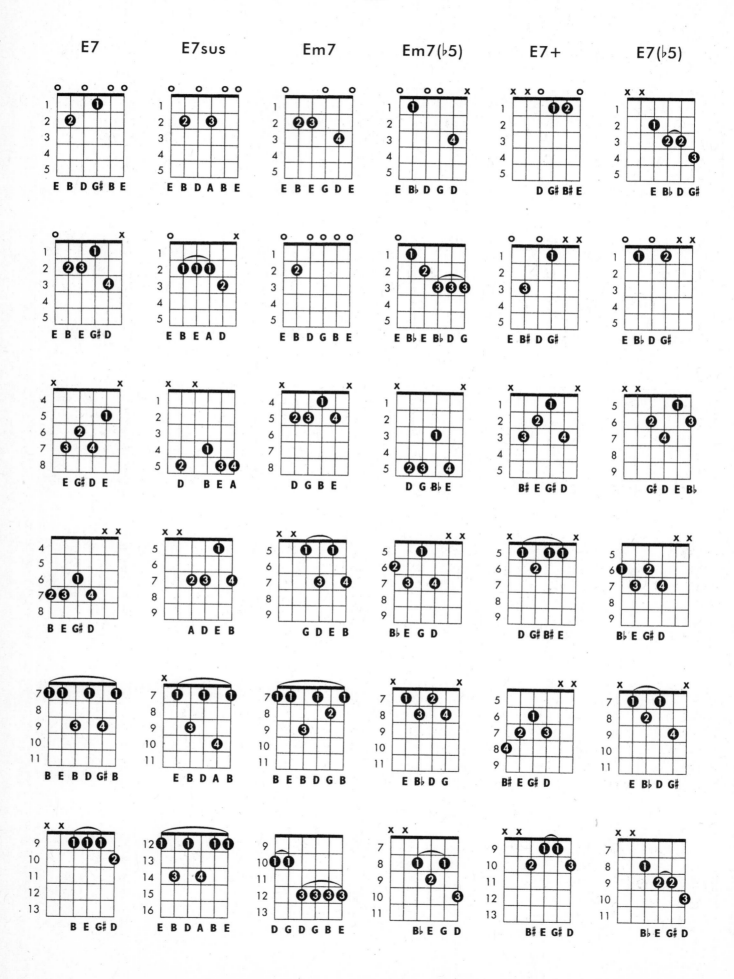

E

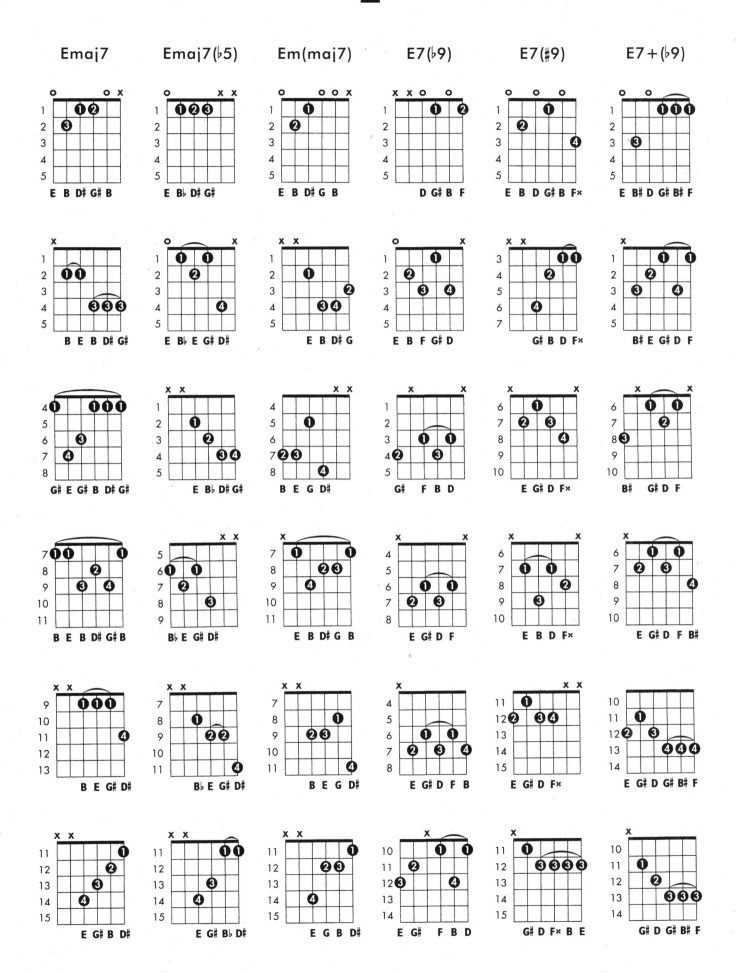

F

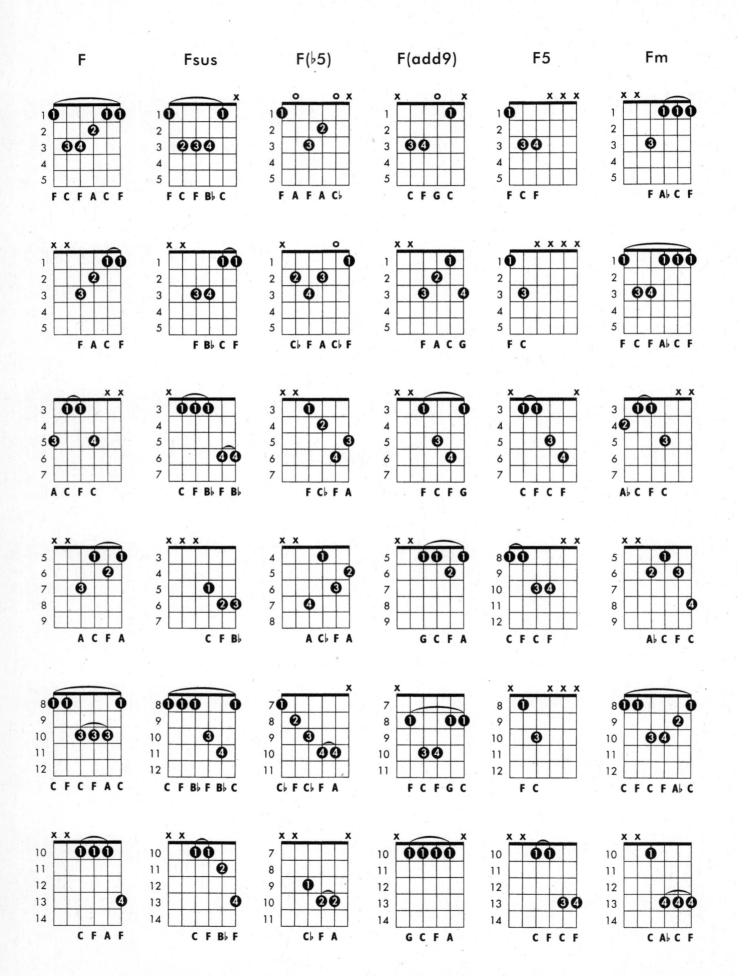

F

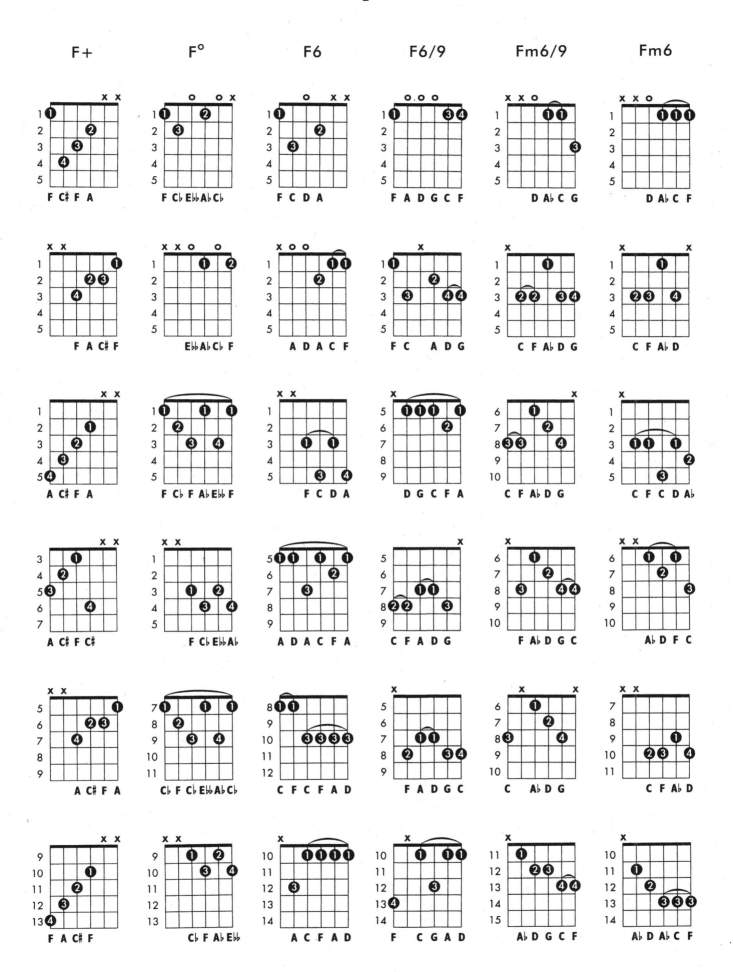

F

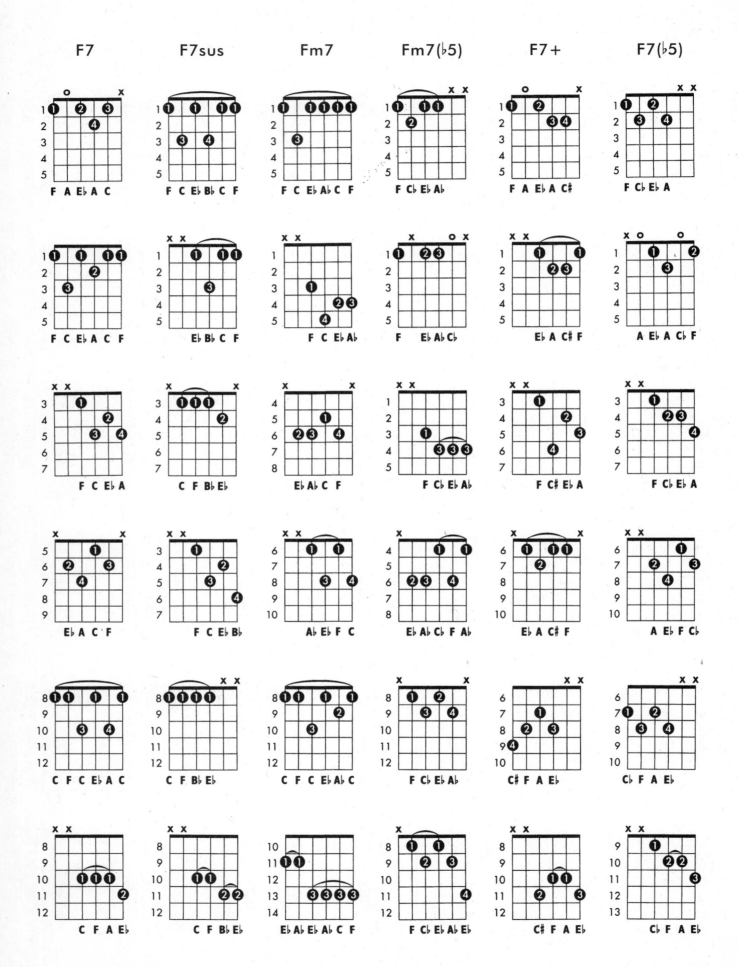

F

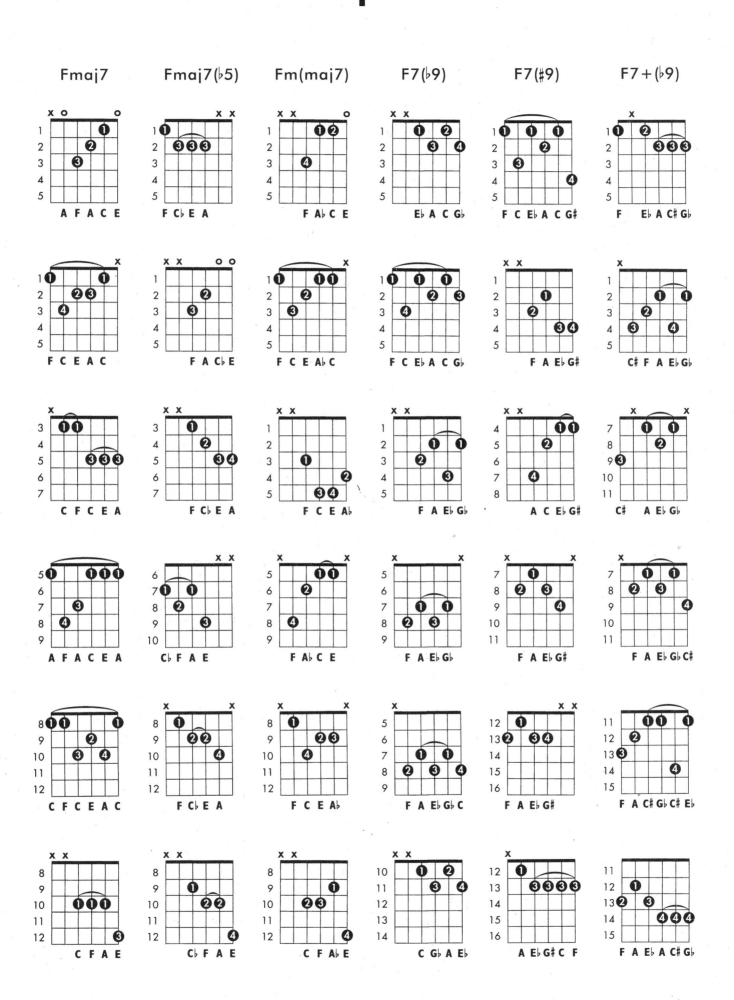

F#

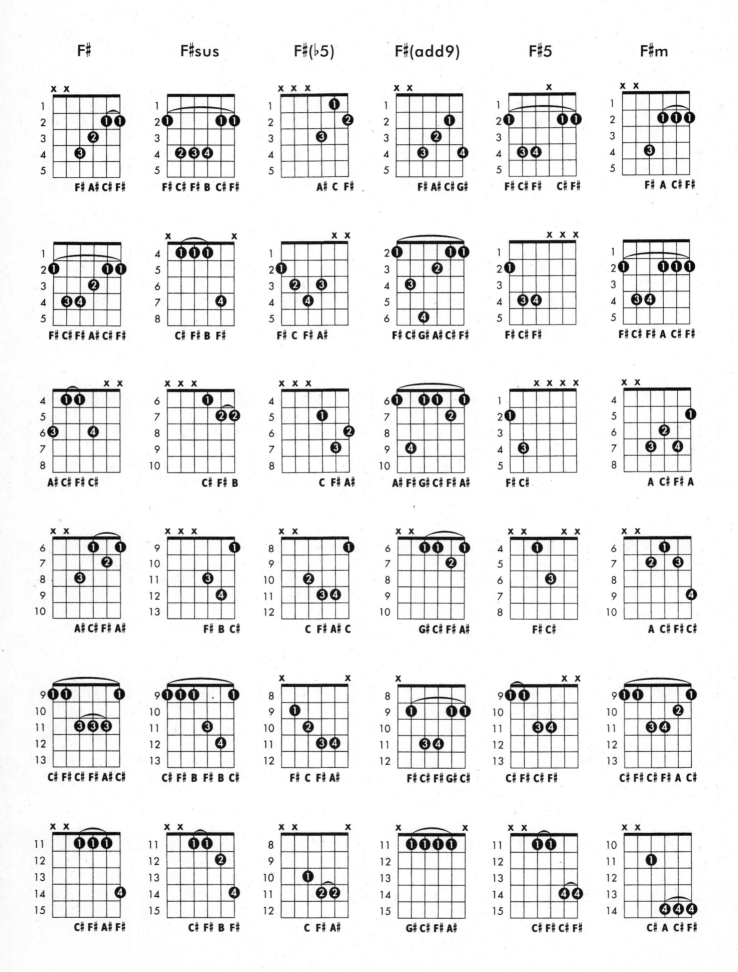

F#

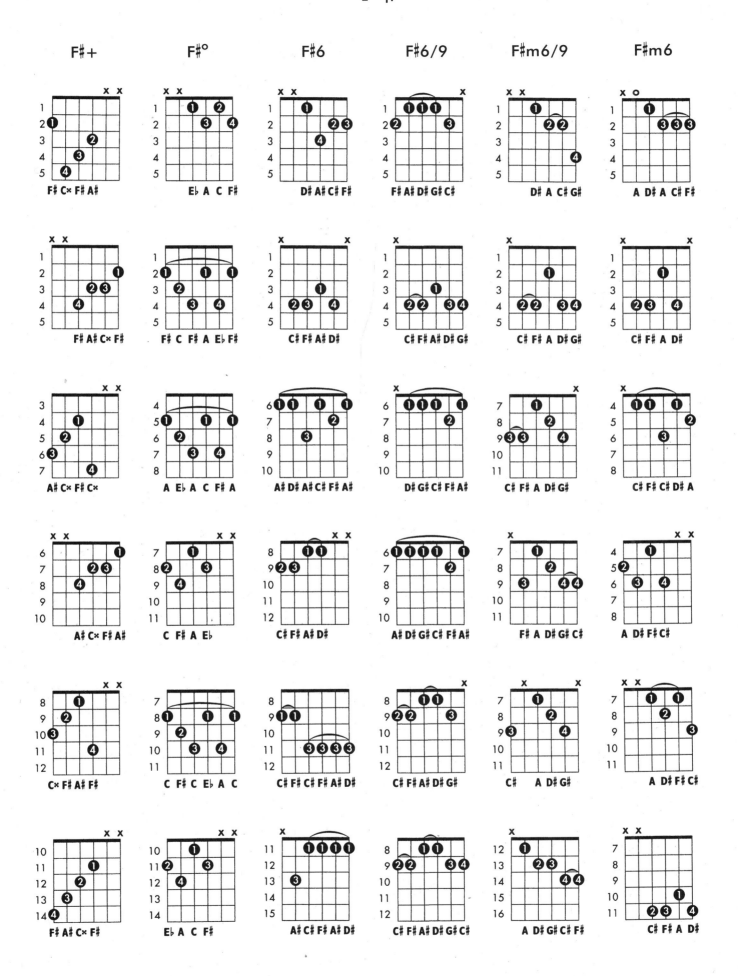

F♯

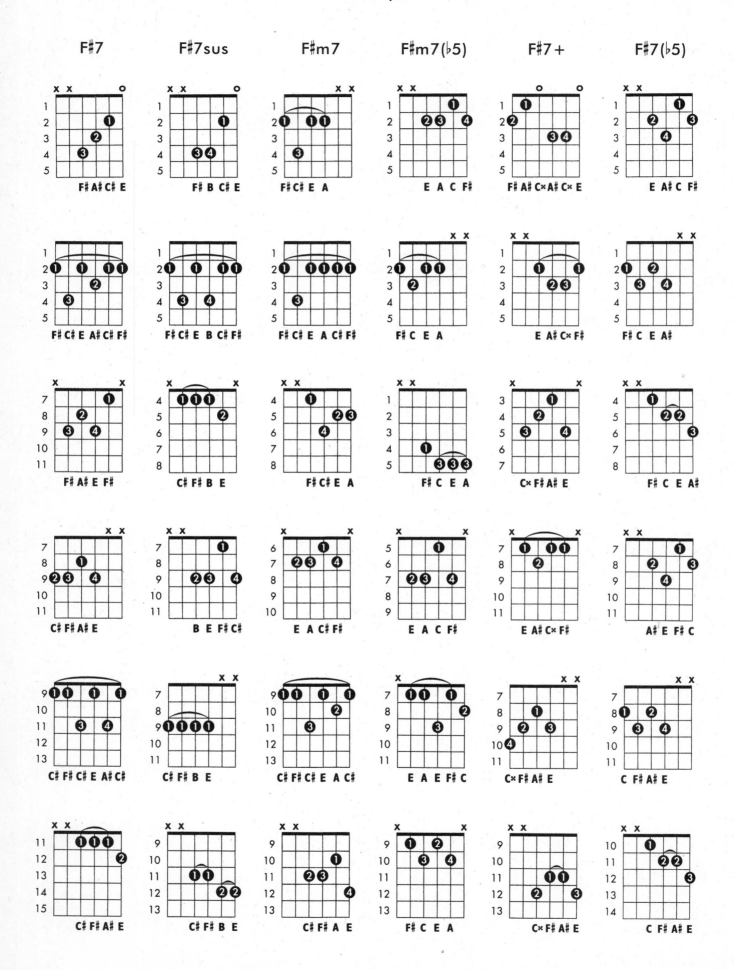

F#

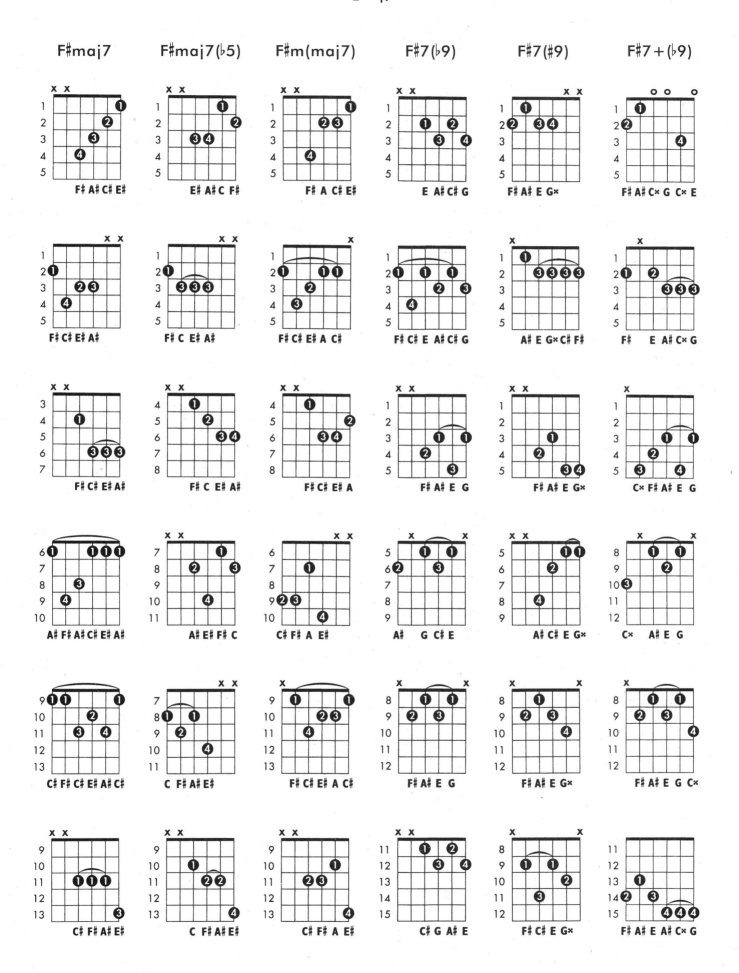

G

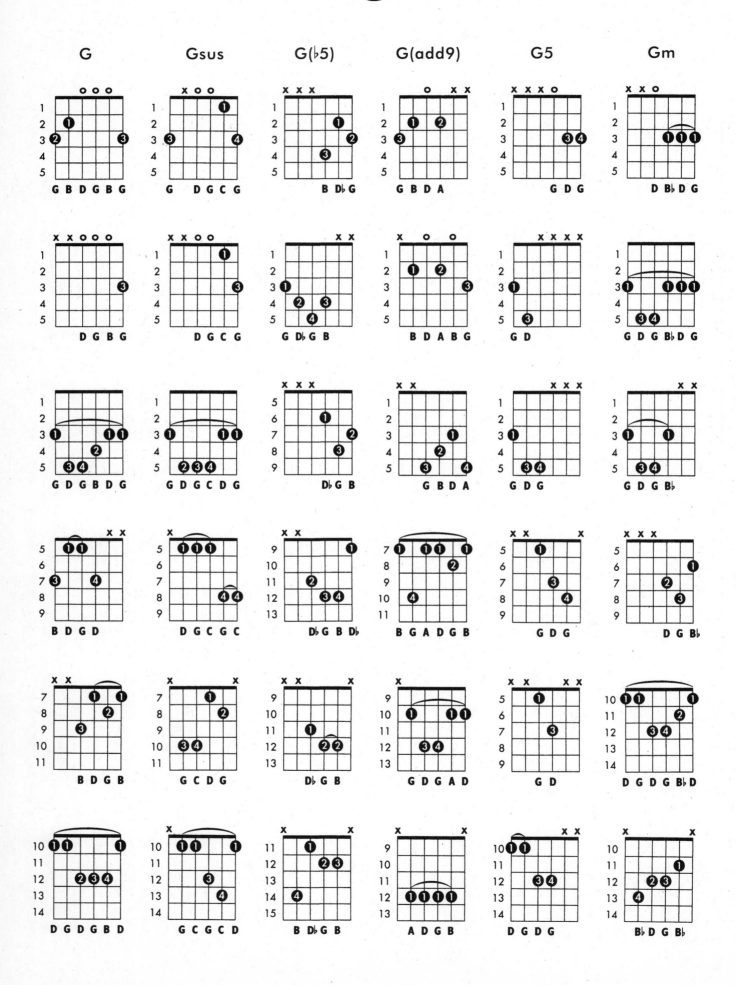

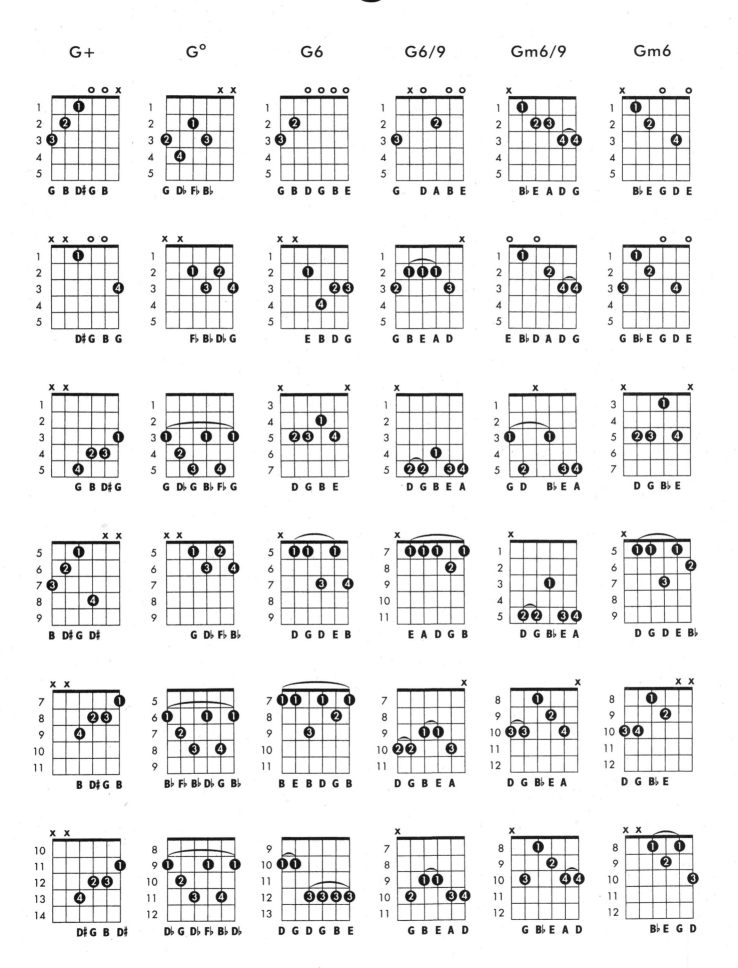

G

G

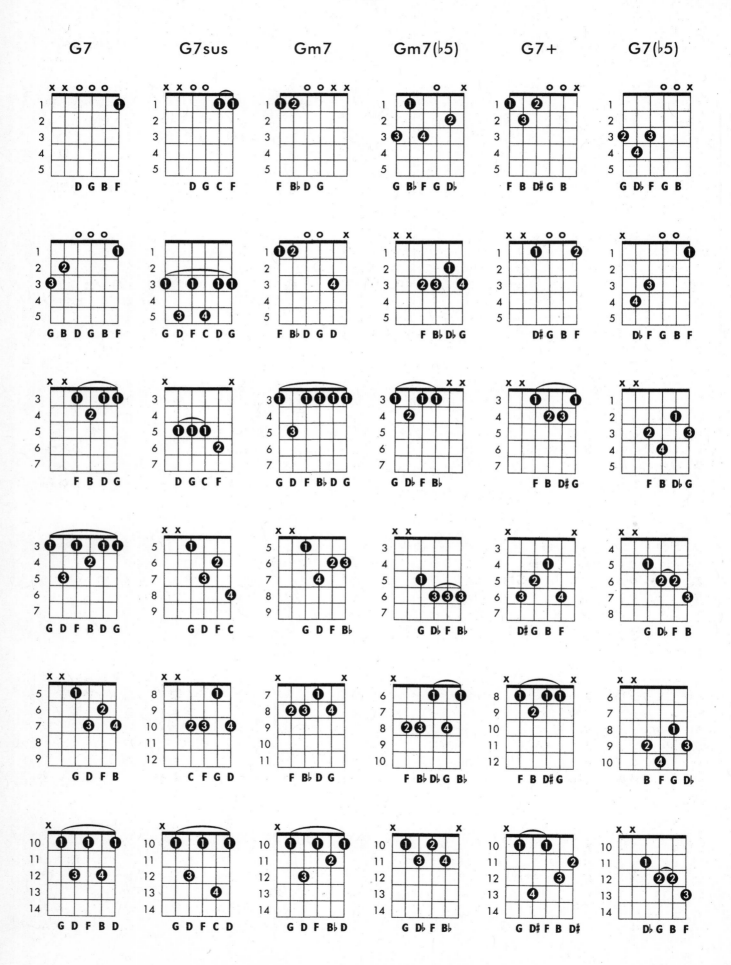

G

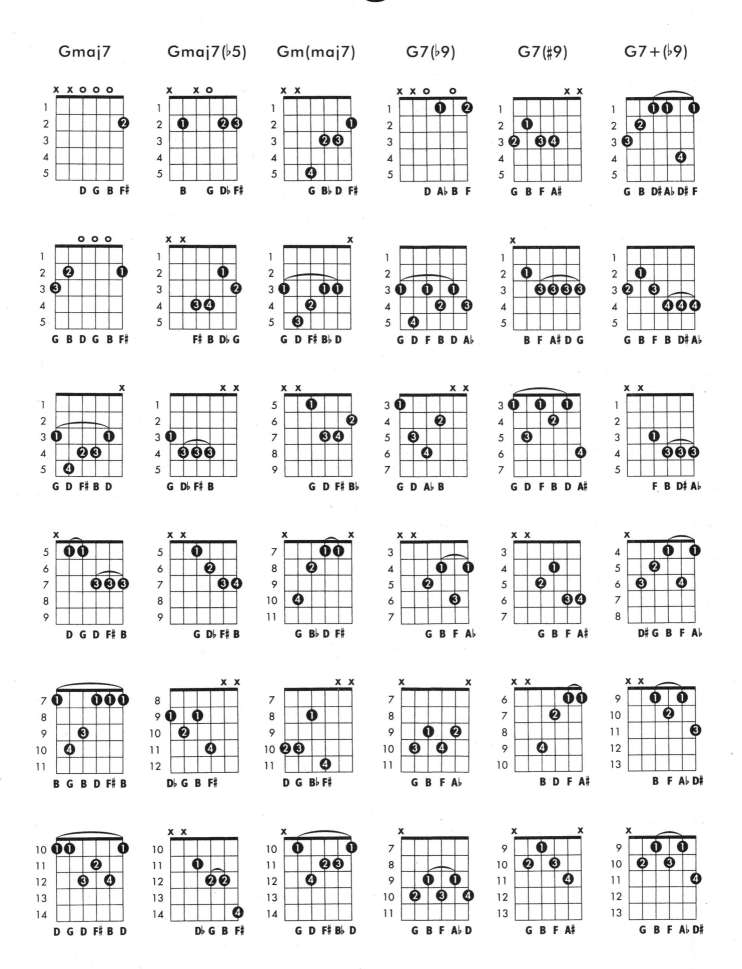

A♭

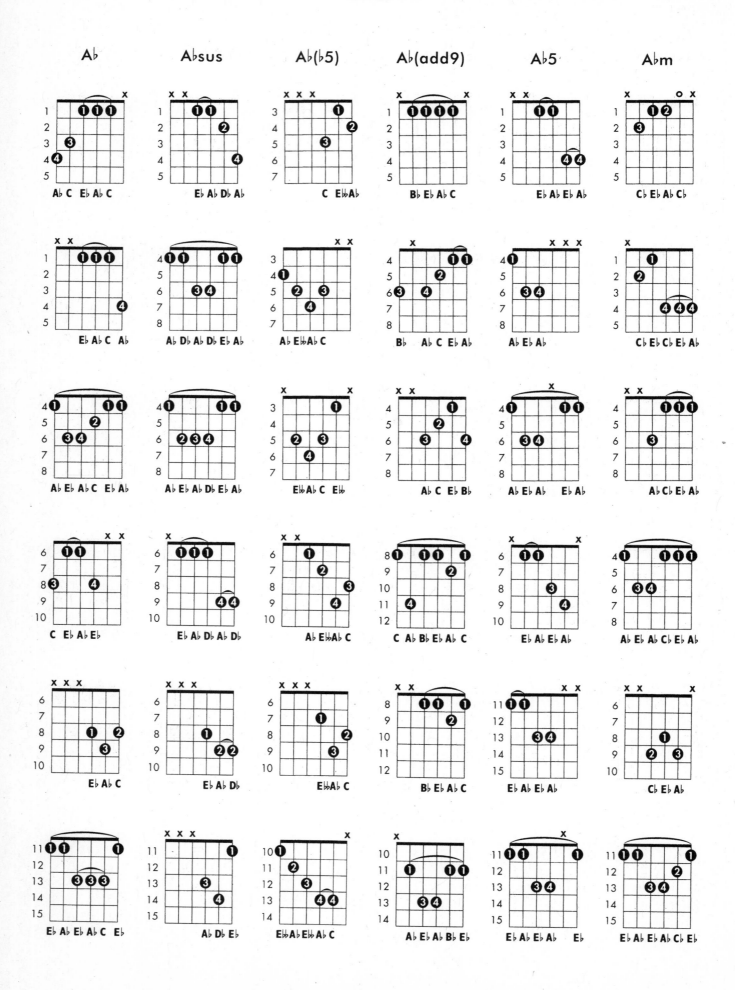

A♭

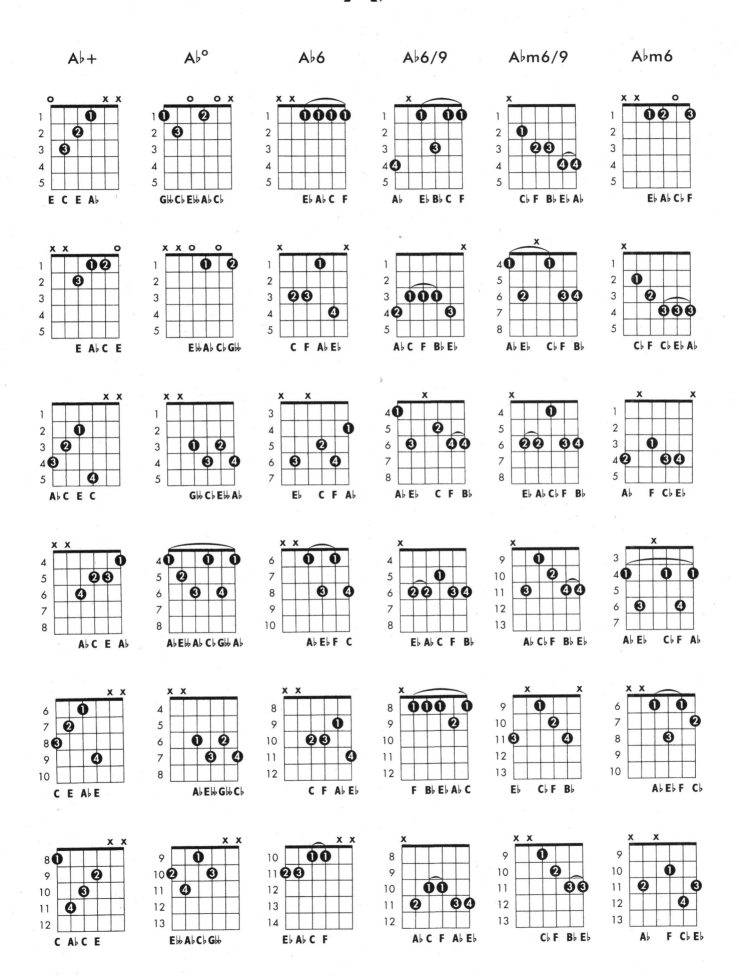

A♭

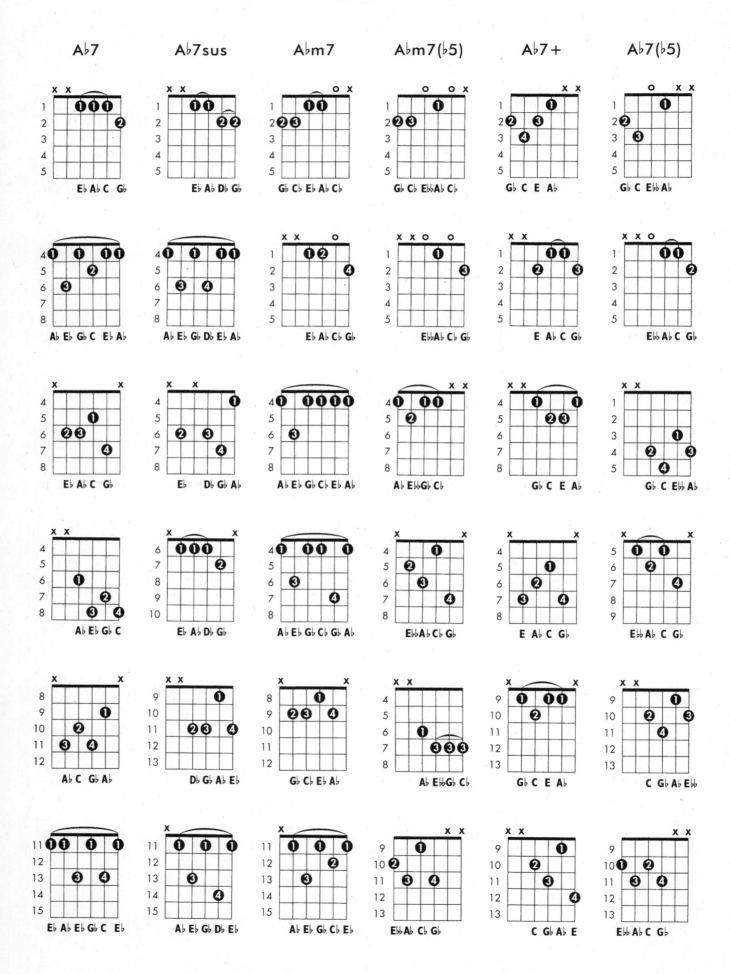

A♭

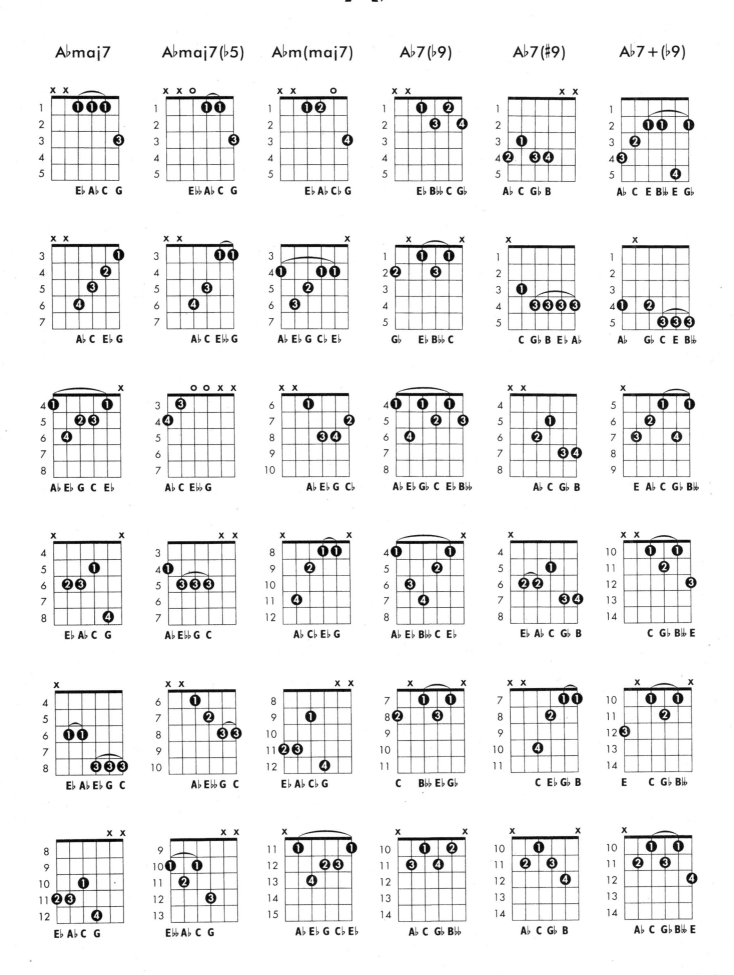

A♭maj7   A♭maj7(♭5)   A♭m(maj7)   A♭7(♭9)   A♭7(♯9)   A♭7+(♭9)

Guitar Fingerboard Chart
Frets 1–12

STRINGS

6th	5th	4th	3rd	2nd	1st
E	A	D	G	B	E

FRETS — **STRINGS**

Fret	6th	5th	4th	3rd	2nd	1st
Open	E	A	D	G	B	E
1st Fret	F	A#/B♭	D#/E♭	G#/A♭	C	F
2nd Fret	F#/G♭	B	E	A	C#/D♭	F#/G♭
3rd Fret	G	C	F	A#/B♭	D	G
4th Fret	G#/A♭	C#/D♭	F#/G♭	B	D#/E♭	G#/A♭
5th Fret	A	D	G	C	E	A
6th Fret	A#/B♭	D#/E♭	G#/A♭	C#/D♭	F	A#/B♭
7th Fret	B	E	A	D	F#/G♭	B
8th Fret	C	F	A#/B♭	D#/E♭	G	C
9th Fret	C#/D♭	F#/G♭	B	E	G#/A♭	C#/D♭
10th Fret	D	G	C	F	A	D
11th Fret	D#/E♭	G#/A♭	C#/D♭	F#/G♭	A#/B♭	D#/E♭
12th Fret	E	A	D	G	B	E

Fingerboard diagram (string note names by fret):

Fret	6th	5th	4th	3rd	2nd	1st
Open	E	A	D	G	B	E
1	F	A#/B♭	D#/E♭	G#/A♭	C	F
2	F#/G♭	B	E	A	C#/D♭	F#/G♭
3	G	C	F	A#/B♭	D	G
4	G#/A♭	C#/D♭	F#/G♭	B	D#/E♭	G#/A♭
5	A	D	G	C	E	A
6	A#/B♭	D#/E♭	G#/A♭	C#/D♭	F	A#/B♭
7	B	E	A	D	F#/G♭	B
8	C	F	A#/B♭	D#/E♭	G	C
9	C#/D♭	F#/G♭	B	E	G#/A♭	C#/D♭
10	D	G	C	F	A	D
11	D#/E♭	G#/A♭	C#/D♭	F#/G♭	A#/B♭	D#/E♭
12	E	A	D	G	B	E